WHO SHOCKED CULTURE?

John Britt has provided change guidance to a number of organizations for over 25 years. He has co-authored *Who Killed Change?*, *Who Pardoned Accountability?*, *Who Kidnapped Excellence?*, *Bee-Come Indispensable* and *What I Really Meant to Say!* Hc has a passion for helping organizations with improved performance.

John is available for keynote speeches and workshops, and can be reached at +1.270.791.2496 or jbritt2468@gmail.com.

Jan Green brings over 25 years of expertise in corporate learning and development, with a focus on leadership growth, team productivity, business professionalism and organizational culture. Her innovative leadership programs have earned recognition from esteemed organizations, including Chief Learning Officer's Learning Elite and the HR.com Leadership Excellence Awards.

Jan is co-author with John Britt on the practical and entertaining book called *Bee-Come Indispensable: 15 Workplace Lessons from the Bees.*

As the founder and owner of Developing You, LLC, Jan partners with leaders to elevate their impact and effectiveness through tailored workshops, on-demand learning solutions and personalized coaching.

Jan can be reached at jan@developingyou.com.

Other books by the authors

Bee-Come Indispensable: 15 Workplace Lessons from the Bees, John Britt and Jan Green

What I Really Meant to Say! A to Z of Meaningful Conversations and Deeper Relationships, John Britt and Vaishakhi Bharucha

WHO SHOCKED CULTURE?

HOW TO MINIMIZE RESISTANCE DURING A BIG CHANGE

JOHN BRITT & JAN GREEN

RUPA

Published by
Rupa Publications India Pvt. Ltd 2025
161-B/4, Gulmohar House,
Yusuf Sarai Community Centre,
New Delhi 110049

Sales centres:
Bengaluru Chennai
Hyderabad Kolkata Mumbai

P-ISBN: 978-93-7003-895-0
E-ISBN: 978-93-7003-428-0

First impression 2025

10 9 8 7 6 5 4 3 2 1

Printed in India

Dedicated to:

Leaders, managers and employees who understand that change can be difficult and have the desire to do it well!

Contents

Foreword

Culture—it can be the architect for successful change, or it can be the scaffolding from which change fails. We often try to reduce our culture to a descriptor:

- We are transparent.
- We are innovative.
- We are inclusive.

Culture is so much more complicated than that. It is much more than 'that's the way we do things here'. In *Who Shocked Culture?*, John Britt and Jan Green have given a voice to Culture at ACME Organization to tell her story and give her perspective on leading and managing change. In this delightful story where the change management and leadership team face the Resistance Family (think Mafia-style family), Culture is at every meeting, every encounter and every communication to exert her influence regarding this next big change that is coming. She has learned so much from a recent change death and she is committed to helping the leaders, managers and employers learn as well so they can successfully overcome this Resistance.

The storyline and dialogue in this narrative are fun. First, you find yourself laughing and then you realize that Culture has just shared a valuable lesson with you.

John and I co-authored *Who Kidnapped Excellence?* As we developed that book, we were both in agreement that if the reader was going to spend his or her valuable time reading a business self-help book, we owed it to them to leave them with thoughts/ideas/strategies/models to help them understand what they might do differently in the future to attain a better outcome. John and Jan have certainly met that objective in *Who Shocked Culture?*

Whether you are a leader, manager or a front-line employee and if you are looking for better performance from yourself and your organization with your changes, read this book, hear Culture's voice, and then look in the mirror to understand what you might do differently in the future to attain a better outcome.

Harry Paul
Co-author of *FISH!* and *Who Kidnapped Excellence?*

Introduction

You may perhaps be wondering why this book, which is about creating successful change, is written from the voice of Culture. That is a very good question, and the answer is quite simple. Culture has a tremendous influence on the chances of success for a big change and yet she is so often misunderstood; an abstraction, influencing our thoughts and actions behind the scenes. If we do not truly recognize her, if we do not call her out for who she is and understand her, how can we learn to lean on her for our change successes?

For many, when Culture comes up, she is reduced to 'that's just the way we do things around here'. But she is much more complex than that. She is formed by leadership, management decisions and behaviors. She matures with failures and successes. She is an accumulation of what has come before her, but more importantly she is a powerful influencer of what is to come in the organization.

There is an old story that you may have heard called *Who Killed Change?* The story ends with the detective providing his summation and opinion of the characters who were culpable in a change death that he was investigating. This story begins as Culture leaves the summation and goes back to her office to contemplate her role, if any, in the death of change. She plugs in her coffee pot and that is where the shock occurs, a *culture shock* that coincides with the introduction of a new big change. She wakes up in the hospital with a new mindset, a new opportunity, and a stronger voice to guide her organization through the challenges that are brought by the Resistance Family.

So, we ask, have your big change journeys been consistently successful?

Have you consistently:

- reached your goals?
- reached your goals in the scheduled time?
- reached your goals on budget?
- communicated consistently and effectively inside the organization?
- experienced too high of an opportunity cost (loss of production, loss of staff, reduced morale)?

As Culture helps navigate her organization through this big change, she leaves us some key points in her diary of what she has learned about change and some thoughts on what we might consider in our own change journey. Whether you are a leader, manager or line employee, we hope Culture's voice reaches you so that your personal and organizational experiences with Change improve.

The Shock

Culture is the deeper level of basic assumptions and beliefs that are shared by members of an organization, that operate unconsciously and define in a basic 'taken for granted' fashion an organization's view of itself and its environment.

—Edgar Schein

Day 1

It was a bright and sunny day. Culture was sitting up in her hospital bed in the step-down unit. Only three days had passed since she had been shocked and almost died but to her it seemed like an eternity. The doctors told her she would live but she would never be the same. A flock of geese flew by in a V-shaped pattern. As she watched them through her window, she reflected back.

A significant Change had been killed at her organization and the Agent had arrived to investigate the murder and interview the suspects, one of which was her. He had spent two days talking with her, Urgency, Vision, Accountability, Sponsorship, Communication, Budget, Performance, Commitment, Powerful Guiding Coalition (PECS), Incentive and others. PECS had earned his nickname because he had a massive upper body from working out his arms and pectoral muscles to hold up the pending changes to the organization but historically had pencil-like legs that kept him from being able to carry the changes out into the organization. Ultimately, Agent had called a meeting of all the suspects, during which, he had, one by one, recounted how each of the suspects was charged with helping Change integrate into the organization and how they had categorically failed to do so. He had ended his meeting with a statement that he did not have enough evidence to arrest any one of the suspects but that he was convinced that the combined effect of the suspects neglecting their responsibilities to Change had caused his death. He had said accusatorily as he looked around the room, 'You are all, each and every one of you, culpable!' The Agent looked slowly around the room accusingly and then he left.

Culture had only stayed at the meeting a few minutes after Agent had gone and she remembered the ensuing discussions with such clarity, it was like she was watching a video clip in slow motion. There had been a moment of silence after Agent closed the door, before Vision opened the conversation. 'I deny any responsibility in Change's death,' she had said emphatically. She surveyed the room and met the gaze of eyes that were accusing, appalled or angry. 'Look,' she went on, 'I'm not saying any of you did it either. I'm just going on record to say I had nothing to do with his death.'

Plan raised his coffee cup in the air and said heartily, 'Here, here'—a gesture of agreement with Vision.

Accountability chimed in with a tone of intense anger. 'That Agent is just blowing smoke. He has nothing to go on. It's the oldest detective trick in the book. He doesn't have enough evidence to accuse anyone, so he accuses everyone. He doesn't get to make an arrest, so he absolves his conscience by pointing his fingers at everyone.'

Incentive broke in, 'Well, maybe Agent's not completely

correct but perhaps he does have a point.'

'You've got to be kidding me,' interrupted Sponsorship.

'No, no, just listen for a minute,' Incentive said. 'I'm not saying any of us, or all of us for that matter, killed Change. I'm just saying that probably all of us could have supported him more. I mean, well, he was new and...' Incentive stopped speaking as Communication began to sob uncontrollably. Performance moved over to sit next to Communication, putting his arm around her and offering her a tissue. Urgency, who had been pacing the room the whole time, left without a word. PECS, who had been sitting on the edge of the table, seemingly staring down at his feet for the whole dialogue, shed a single large tear that hit the floor. Budget, who sat next to Culture on the couch, had not moved or uttered a word but looked as if she had been shot by a stun gun. Commitment was noticeably missing.

Culture left the room shortly after Urgency did. For the first time in years, she was confused. Her role in the organization had never been challenged. She was a charter member of ACME organization and considered herself to be the chief architect of the values the organization had adopted. Over time, her influence had molded the basic assumptions and beliefs the organization had about itself. Although publicly she conveyed a deep sense of humility, privately she knew that her presence had a profound impact on the work behaviors of most of the people who worked here.

Once in her office, she pulled her diary from her drawer and wrote:

'Could I have been wrong about my influence? Not the presence of it—that's a given, but of the ultimate effect? Have I played a part in laying a foundation here that is so rigid that those leaders and managers in that room can rationalize forsaking Change? What is my true role here?'

She paused for a few moments, then began writing again. 'Just as personality and character guides the actions of a person, I—Culture—am capable of guiding the actions of a group, perhaps even the whole organization. I must reevaluate my role with future Changes.'

She knew it was going to be a long night and decided to make a pot of coffee. As she was plugging in the coffee pot, she thought, 'When the next Change gets here, I'm going to...'

There was a flash of light, and everything went black.

The Resistance Family

Day 2

Resistance had been busy. He had not survived this long by just being passive. Within two days of Agent's meeting and Culture's shock, he had assembled his family in his lair to plan for the failure of a new Change that would come. And come he would. It could be weeks, months or years but a new Change would come, and they must be ready for him. Resistance considered any Change a waste: of time, of energy, of resources. Resistance smiled remembering the times acquaintances had asked him what line of business he was in, and he simply had replied, 'Waste management'.

So that everyone was clear on who they were to focus on, Resistance had placed an organizational chart on the wall. Next to each of the members of the Change team, Resistance placed the names of the persons on his team who he considered their nemeses:

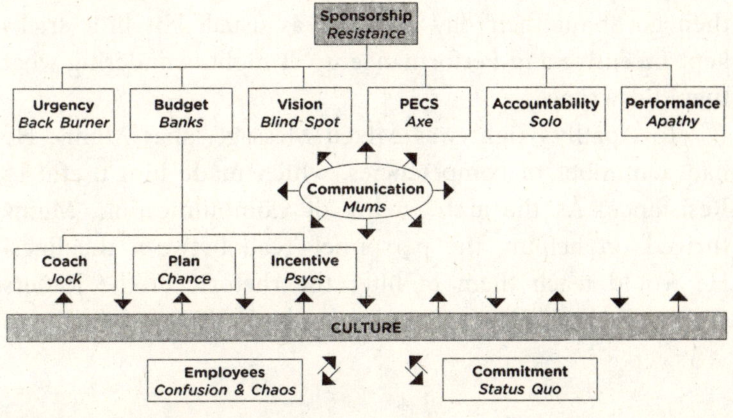

Resistance looked around the room and table with a sense of pride that could be likened to a mob boss at the head of the dinner table entertaining his prize soldiers. Immediately to his right was Ego, alias Solo. His primary strength was convincing those people who were being asked by Change to alter their work behaviors or habits that they did not need any outside help. He helped them understand that they made it to where they were primarily on their own, that they knew their operations better than anyone, and that outside help by Change and his gang was unwanted and un-needed. Solo proudly asserted himself as the nemesis of Accountability. Resistance noted that, as always, Solo looked fit and was well tailored.

Sitting to Solo's right—and at first impression seeming to be the antithesis of Solo—was Apathy. Apathy was overweight, dressed sloppily, and obviously had not shaved for a few days. His appearance had not, however, dissuaded Resistance from enlisting and keeping him in the family. He knew Apathy was a master of convincing personnel that the upper echelon of the organization did not care about them, so why should they care about Change? Resistance chuckled to himself as he thought about Apathy's favorite technique—the PA as he called it, passive aggressiveness. He would teach the personnel to act like they were embracing what Change was offering but then go about their day, business as usual. His little tricks kept Incentive and Performance up at night, wondering what they did wrong.

To Apathy's right was Mixed Message, alias Mums. He had a number of competencies, which made him useful to Resistance. As the arch enemy of Communication, Mums thrived on helping the personnel 'read between the lines'. He would teach them to filter the rhetoric of the leaders and managers and examine the residual message, which was usually, in Mum's opinion, self-serving. Gossip was another one of Mum's favorite tools. He could distract Change from moving forward on an initiative for weeks at a time with this technique. Resistance noticed that, as usual, Mums had his hand cupped over someone's ear and was 'passing along a message'.

The 'someone' that was sitting to Mum's right was known as Back Burner or BB. He never got in a hurry. He prided himself on being the source of Urgency's constant pacing. He was artful in creating roadblocks that prevented leaders and managers from moving quickly on something Change needed. One of his favorite techniques was meetings. Of course, BB had to share the limelight with Mums on this one. They would plant the seeds that meetings were needed to discuss the things Change wanted to do and then, well, Mums would do his thing. BB was also known for throwing out Culture's name when the leaders and managers were getting close to making a decision that Change needed from them. He would intone negatively, 'Is this going to be consistent with our Culture and our values?' He would facilitate the conversation until the leaders and managers began taking opposing positions and then he would go on a coffee break. His work was done for the day.

Directly opposite of Resistance at the round table was Blind Spot. With a patch over his right eye, jet-black hair in a ponytail and a short black beard, Blind Spot reminded Resistance of a pirate. Years before, Blind Spot had confided to Resistance that he was actually one year away from becoming an optometrist when a bizarre accident had caused him to lose his right eye. Embittered, he decided to dedicate his life to impairing the Vision of organizations. Resistance smiled as he recalled the day Blind Spot had altered the concavity of Vision's glasses when they had been left lying on his desk.

Next to Blind Spot was Division, alias Axe. Axe was powerfully built. He was six feet eight inches, weighed 350-plus pounds and was all muscle. To add emphasis to his features, he always dressed like Paul Bunyon. But Resistance knew that it was not his stature which brought value to this family, but his finesse. Axe's core competency was polarization. Resistance was convinced Axe could persuade a Democrat to vote for a Republican, and vice versa. He was skilled at helping the team focus on the pros and cons of a decision and persuading different team members to take opposite positions on the issue, to the degree that no one could come up with a compromise or a win-win agreement. Every time the Family came together, Axe bragged about how he had wrestled PECS that week and had pinned him so easily because PECS's legs were so weak.

Demotivator sat to Axe's right. A long-time friend of Apathy, Demotivator was known to the group as Psychs. Psychs had actually purchased a PhD in Psychology from an internet-based virtual college and although everyone was aware that he was not a bona fide psychologist, Psychs was truly gifted in helping the personnel see the downside of what Change was promoting. His self-proclaimed personal mission was to stay two steps ahead of Incentive. His two favorite tools were doubt and mistrust. Apathy once accused Psychs of hypnotizing the personnel. Psychs just smiled and said, 'You know a lack of trust can be a strong hypnotic.'

Banks sat next to Psychs. His role was to keep Budget at the extremes. So far, he had done a good job. Spring-boarding off Culture's proclivity toward conservatism, he had subconsciously kept Budget from letting go of needed funds for helping Change. Normally, Banks dressed very conservatively. Today, however, he wore an expensive suit, a Rolex and a variety of gold jewelry. Resistance had called Banks before the meeting to explain that in light of Agent's directive for Budget to support Change's financial needs and Budget's perceived response, Banks might need to alter his strategy and get Budget to swing to the opposite extreme of overspending, which could hurt the organization as much as underspending. Resistance saw Bank's attire as a symbol of his acceptance of this new strategy.

Next to Banks were Confusion and Chaos—fraternal twins. Resistance did not consider these two to be major gang members but rather 'worker bees' for the rest of the Family to do their bidding. Confusion and Chaos were well aware of their status and did not seem to care. They were younger and less mature than everyone else and were constantly up and down from the table picking at one another and at the members of the Family. While this activity perturbed Resistance for the purposes of his meeting, he tolerated the interruption because he knew that these two met a need of his—in the ACME organization—that was on a different level than the rest of his team.

The next seat was held by Chance. Characteristically, he played methodically with a pair of dice. Every now and then he would roll them out on the table. No one knew his methodology but his reactions once the dice landed were dramatic and generally swung from beating his fists angrily on the table to an unbridled scream of pleasure. When called in by Resistance, Chance's work centered on distracting Plan. Resistance knew that Chance had a number of 'tricks up his sleeves'. One of his favorites was keeping Plan focused on strategy—the big picture. He knew Plan's proclivity for 'flying high in the clouds' and he did all he could to prevent Plan from coming down to focus on the tactical action items that were necessary for a successful change. When it came to managing Plan, Resistance knew he could leave it to Chance.

Next to Chance sat Jock. One look at Jock and one could tell he was a true athlete. If his lean, muscular build did not give it away, the fact that he always wore a baseball shirt and carried a baseball bat with him did. Jock was one of the pure-bred athletes and everything came easily to him. He had once said to Resistance, 'Practice? Ha—I don't need to practice. Let's just get out there and play.' Jock had come to despise Trainer. Trainer always wanted him and the team to learn something new. He didn't need to learn something new. He was already a star. Why should he change? Thus, over time, Jock had mentally associated Trainer and Change as adversaries. Now older, he had found his vocation in working with the Resistance crew to fight Trainer and Change.

Notably, to Resistance's immediate left was an empty chair. This chair was sporadically occupied by Fear. Fear was the senior-most member of Resistance's team and was believed to come or not come to these called meetings as a symbol of his veteran status. The truth was that Fear was an enigma even to Resistance. It was not so much a question of loyalty for Resistance but more so of effectiveness. In the old days, Fear's track record for impeding Change was solid. And even to date, he maintained a decent record. But in the last few years, Resistance had noticed a subtle difference. The same competencies and tactics Fear used to intimidate people to resist Change, in a few cases, had actually created the opposite effect. The Fear he brought them seemingly caused them to embrace Change.

And where was he now? Why wasn't he here? Resistance could not wait any longer. He pounded his gavel on the table and called the meeting to order.

Although the Resistance Family was not 'top of mind' for Culture as she lay in her hospital bed, Resistance was not new to her. It would only be a few days before she was prompted to revisit her diary to review some of her entries about Resistance from some years ago.

Dear Diary, (Previous lesson learned: Change is personal.)

It is very easy to underestimate the amount of resistance that can be ignited by a new change. In fact, resistance to change isn't always visible—at least at first. The resistance may start small, with a quiet undercurrent of individuals trying to make sense of the new change. The important fact that 'change initiators' often forget is that change is personal. Change initiators often think about how the change is going to impact the organization, improve the business and grow the bottom line, but those on the front line who have to implement the change often think first about what this change means to them personally.

The first thing people often think is how it is going to affect them. There is often a lightning-quick silent response of, 'What am I going to have to give up? What will I lose with this new change?' Even if the change will bring positive results in efficiency, improved workflow, better customer service, the default thoughts for many are: 'Will this change disrupt my current comfort level in my job, will it require me to change the way I have been working, and could this change be a threat to my security in the organization?' A natural default to change is that this change will take something from me, I will lose something, or I will have to give up something because of it.

Dear Diary, (Lesson learned: Resistance will grow stronger with more members.)

Another lesson learned in the past about resistance is that Resistance likes company. In a changing environment, some individuals may subtly assess the readiness for change in others, and for those who feel the fear, or are angry about it, they may unite together in their stance against it. These feelings may be very quiet and not noticeable in the beginning, but like-minds against change may fuel a common mission against it and can become a strong force.

Dear Diary, (Lesson learned: Intentional observation and active-listening are important skills to detect early challenges with change.)

Over the years, I have learned that resistance exists everywhere—in all types of organizations. How will we know if resistance is alive in our organization? We should begin by watching and listening. We can watch behaviors and see how individuals respond to change. Are they engaged? Are they demonstrating the needed behaviors that will move the organization forward? Do they embrace new initiatives and continuously keep learning to be ready for the next change? Or do we sometimes see:

- Procrastination and half-hearted measures.
- Initial bursts of activity and energy that end up fizzling into unproductive or nonvalue-added behaviors.
- A lack of total commitment, involvement of the key stakeholders and new initiatives are only being driven by a few.
- More 'Talking the Talk, versus Walking the Walk'.
- Watch what is happening behind the scenes—

providing important communications, keeping people up to date with new information, regular one-on-one coaching, assessing the readiness of the team for change, and addressing any concerns that exist.

- Is there a spirit of learning, growth and continuous development in your organization?
- Are leaders demonstrating that they are advocates of the new change? Are they positive, encouraging and supportive? Are they continuing to hone their own skills so they can lead by example?

The second area of focus is listening. Listen to the words that are being said by individuals at all levels.

- Do leaders work closely with their teams and ask for feedback, ask questions and respond to concerns?
- In the breakroom or in passing conversations, do we hear negative comments about the speed of change and the impact on workers? Sometimes individuals have been pulled into the Resistance Family, and they are not even aware until they hear themselves carrying forward the resistance message to others. Do our leaders ask about and encourage continuous development to be prepared for the next important change?
- Is our organization making an effort to ask and listen to the employees who many times are the essential technical experts who will be asked to help roll these changes out? Are we using focus groups to ask important questions and listen to their thoughts, concerns and ideas?
- An important precursor to listening is providing important information upfront, openly, quickly,

consistently and honestly.

- Is our organization talking about the important role of change in our regular communications?
- Is our communication siloed to an important few, or sent to the entire organization?
- Are we asking the right questions to inspire innovative thought that moves us beyond the status quo?

Dear Diary, (Lesson learned: All types of change can trigger resistance. Even the most positive change can trigger resistance if we do not discuss the change openly and help people journey through it.)

Today I am remembering that there are <u>many faces of change</u> that can call up the different characters of the Resistance Family. Here are some of them, where resistance has emerged in full force:

- A new process, software, or procedure that may impact a single department, or even the entire organization.
- A new initiative that may impact the way the organization operates, communicates or serves the client.
- The change could be a new niche, or a newly created function that is an imperative to stay current, relevant and meet the future needs of customers.
- The change could be a merger or an acquisition where cultures collide, and chaos (resistance) could reign with abandon if not managed carefully.
- Sometimes the change can be a new position or role that is responsible for making important improvements to the organization. It is very important to be aware of resistance in this situation. In situations like this,

resistance can be focused on not only the message but also the messenger.

And finally, there are simple but effective things all employees can do to stay positive and avoid getting captured by the Resistance Family. Here are some important tips:

1. Walk the talk of being an advocate for important changes that will help the organization succeed and thrive.
2. Encourage others to give this new change an opportunity to succeed. Explain that we can go through this journey as a team, department or organization. The objective will be easier to accomplish together.
3. Even in the toughest moments, seek to stay positive. Talk about successes, lessons learned, growth, and the *why* behind the change.
4. Remind individuals (and ourselves) that we have been through many changes in the past and we will soon be on the other side of this as well.
5. Many times, we 'fear the unknown' of changes, which seems to open the door to the Resistance Family, but in reality, we should fear 'lack of change' because this could impact our ability to survive in the future.
6. Campaign for and communicate the importance of change. So many people fear change, but what can we do to make change our competitive advantage? We need to speak the value of change and help others see the same—not to fear it.
7. The Resistance Family professes to be the protectors of the culture. On the contrary, they are culture killers. The unique attributes of a great culture are clear vision, positivity, innovation, creativity, curiosity and outstanding client service. In order for all of the culture ingredients to

exist, the following items need to be a part of the current culture:

a. We must focus on continuous improvement and a mission for making things better for our clients and the organization.
b. We must help create a culture that is not only willing to change but is also focused on change to stay current and meet future needs of clients.
c. There must be an alignment between the vision, values and goals of the organization, departments and employees.
d. Professional development must be a high priority to continuously upskill and be prepared for the next change opportunity.

Fear Speaks

Day 3

Culture was in that limbo state where she knew she was trying to pull herself out of a deep sleep. Her last thoughts had been about her being shocked before she had drifted off to sleep in her hospital bed. When she finally managed to wake, Culture looked to her right and the dim light from the window told her it was dusk. Hearing a slight rustle of cloth, she turned her head to the left and startled. Sitting next to her bed in a chair was Fear.

Fear was on the edge of his chair, elbows on his knees and hands clasped in front of him. He said softly, 'How are you?'

Again, Culture was startled. She had seen Fear off and on around the organization for years, but she had not once heard him speak. Still a bit confused, she replied, 'Okay, I guess.' A short period of uncomfortable silence passed before she finally said,

'What are you doing here?'

'You called for me?' Fear answered serenely.

'Called for you?' she questioned. 'I didn't call for you.'

With a hint of a smile, he said, 'Well, yes you did, but not consciously. No one really ever calls me consciously, but your subconscious undeniably placed the call.'

'But I don't understand,' stated Culture with a prodding look on her face.

Fear offered, 'Everyone has me around—some more than others. Some people pretend I don't exist but sooner or later they know. I don't always make a visible appearance but that does not mean I'm not there. I think I have a reputation that leans toward the negative, but I can be positive for people. I'm a free agent, you know.'

'Free agent?' she enquired.

'Yes, a free agent. When I am called, I don't come with an agenda. I come to serve the needs of those who called me. Take baseball for example. Do you like baseball?'

Culture just stared at him blankly.

Fear continued, 'One batter is on deck waiting his turn to bat, and he calls me. He only calls for enough of me to balance his confidence. He uses me as a guard against overzealousness. I remind him that he is a skilled hitter who has faced better pitchers in the past but to watch out for this pitcher's slider. Another batter on deck calls me, again subconsciously, wanting me there in person. He needs reminding that he is inept and his greatest successes this time at bat might be a foul ball. People use me how they choose to use me. They have free will and I am a free agent.'

'So why did I call you?' asked Culture with interest.

'Aha!' replied Fear with emphasis. 'Based on what I just told you, am I qualified or positioned to answer that for you?'

'Well, no. I guess not.'

'So, think then. Think deeply. Why do you need me here?'

Culture reflected on the last several days. Change had been killed—murdered. After his investigation, Agent had accused the majority of the leadership and management team of complicity in the death by means of negligence. Up until this moment, she had not admitted any personal culpability but now she thought, 'Could I have anything to do with Change's death? Am I so entrenched in the values and tradition of the organization that I have created a blind spot for Change?'

Fear watched with great interest as she introspected. At last, he knew by her facial expressions that she was coming to the conclusion of why she had called for him. As tears came to her eyes, she said to him, 'I'm guilty. I killed Change.'

'Well then,' replied Fear. 'Now we both know why I'm here. I sense though that you've not asked me here to remind you that a foul ball is going to be your best outcome, but that, instead, you've got a decent track record and that you can face the challenges ahead so you can hit his slider.'

'His slider?' questioned Culture.

Fear dodged the question by saying, 'Look, you didn't kill Change all by yourself. There were a lot of people involved, and I might label it more like…involuntary manslaughter, not murder.'

'Thank you,' said Culture, but Fear's tactic had not worked. 'Whose slider?' she demanded.

'Resistance.'

'What does he want?' she said urgently.

'I'm not trying to be coy here,' Fear replied. Culture noticed that Fear appeared to be fading, becoming translucent. 'But I must remind you that I am a free agent and I'm not at liberty to divulge to others why people call me.' Fear considered whether he should mention what was self-evident to himself. He decided the timing was right. 'Suffice it to say that you can expect another Change to come and well, I…' Fear faded away.

For a fleeting moment, Culture considered pinching herself to make sure she wasn't dreaming but the reality of this strange conversation soon returned to her. She considered the power of the subconscious. Culture pulled the diary from under her pillow that Budget had thoughtfully brought her and wrote.

Dear Diary,

I think I remember the key points the professor in college had tried to teach me about myself. I wish I had my notes that I saved but I will write what I can for now without them. The professor was quoting Ed Schein, who said something like this: 'Culture is a pattern of shared tacit assumptions that was learned by a group as it solved its problems of external adaptation and internal integration that has worked well enough to be considered valid, and, therefore, to be taught to the new members as the correct way to perceive, think and feel in relation to those problems.'

I remember at the time that he wrote on the board how complex it seemed to be. Our assignment was to break down the quote and find out what it meant to each class member. I did the assignment this way:

Culture—that's me.

- I am the result of a pattern. I am not the result of any one event but instead, I have been formed by repeated assumptions and experiences over time.
- I am the result of sharing. I am the result of what the members of my organization have learned as we have evolved. And I cannot forget or dismiss shared 'tacit assumptions'. I am not the result of announcements or proclamations. I am a product of experiences and their outcomes that has happened insidiously over time.
- I am the result of problem solving. As the members of my organization have solved problems of both internal integration and external adaption that have arisen, my nature has been formed.
- I am the result of reinforcement. As members solve these problems, the methods that have been successful

are passed on to new members as a yardstick for how they should behave within the organization.

- Culture picked up the hand mirror that was lying on her bedside table. She looked at her reflection. She adjusted the mirror so she could see herself and write her thoughts at the same time:
- I provide structure and meaning to my organization.
- I set the tone and provide the guardrails for the acceptable behaviors here.
- I am the backstop to the values that we espouse.
- Essentially, just as people have unique personalities, I represent the personality of this organization.

As she sipped her coffee, decaffeinated by order of her doctor, the cup slipped a bit in her hand. In her effort to correct her grip, she knocked the hand mirror over. She heard the unmistakable cracking sound. When she turned the mirror over and looked at herself, she was astounded. The mirror, indeed, had multiple cracks. She saw herself clearly in the center but in the fragments of the cracked pieces, she thought she could see others. She looked up at her intravenous drip and wondered what they may have put in it to cause this hallucination. She looked back at the mirror, and saw the faces of her leadership team, each occupying a fragment of the mirror. She turned the mirror slightly and the faces were replaced by multiple employees of the organization. She put down the mirror and shook her head as if shaking something off from her hair. Culture took a deep breath and then picked the mirror back up.

It was just her again and somehow, she now had a better understanding of her synthesis and symbiosis with the organization. She began to write again:

Could I, while I was asleep, actually have called for Fear? If so, was it because of Change's murder or because of my near-death experience from the electrocution? Or could it be a little of both? And this Resistance, I know of him. Not that I have ever met him—or his gang, for that matter—but their antics and influence are known far and wide in organizations. Watch out for his slider. That's what Fear had said. Watch out for his slider.

It came to her. Resistance and his gang were at ACME organization right now and she was pretty sure she knew why.

The Big Change

Day 7

After several days in the hospital, Culture took a few more days at home before returning to work the following Monday. She was welcomed back with enthusiasm by those on the leadership team who happened to run into her. She noted the excitement in the air and soon learned of the source. Communication informed her that Sponsorship had called a meeting. Usually in situations like this virtually everyone usually knew about the news before the formal announcement was made, but not this time.

By 10:00 a.m., everyone was gathered in the leadership breakroom, the same room where Agent had held his meeting with them to describe how he thought each of them had played a part in killing Change. Even Urgency, who was notorious for being late, was there. Although he was pacing back and forth across the back of the room and frequently consulting his wristwatch, he had actually made it on time. Communication was sitting at one of the randomly placed tables in the room, looking confused. Culture thought it was most likely because of the mysterious nature of the meeting. For most meetings, Communication at least had a good idea of what was going to be discussed, but not this one.

Vision, in predictable fashion, stood with her back to the group looking out the window. From where Culture was standing, she could see her profile and thought there was something different about Vision. She kept putting her hand to the side of her face and then back down to her side. It came to her. 'Glasses,' she thought. 'She doesn't have her glasses on.' Culture got her attention, put her right and left forefingers to her temples and mouthed, 'Glasses?' Vision grinned slightly, not a common occurrence for her, and pointed to her own face and mouthed back, 'Laser surgery.' Culture grinned a little too and nodded her head in understanding.

Incentive was sitting on one of the couches alone, dressed in a solid black pantsuit. Communication has said that since Change's death she had worn black every day. Culture knew that Incentive had gotten close to Change in the six months he was here, and she had taken his death pretty hard. Sitting at a table with Performance was Accountability. They were engaged in a deep conversation about something as they leaned over and intermittently pointed to what looked like a large set of blueprints, although Culture could not be sure that that was what it was.

Budget was sitting on the couch in the room. When Culture saw her, she thought, 'She does not look good. Not good at all.' Because she was sitting, it was difficult to tell for sure, but Culture thought she looked like she had lost weight and there were definitely bags under her eyes. In contrast, PECS was a picture of health. He was making his way around the room joking with everyone trying to lift their spirits.

The door opened slightly, and Sponsorship entered the room. He held the handle with the door half opened, stuck his head back out the door, whispered something not discernable to the people in the room, and then entered fully. After surveying his surroundings to check off that everyone was there, he began.

'Thank you for coming on such short notice and might I say,' inclining his head toward Culture, 'it is certainly good to have Culture back in our midst.' After a light round of clapping, he continued. 'This team knows full well that the last couple of weeks have been extremely difficult.' Incentive blew her nose into a tissue. 'We all could spend a good deal of our time looking back and second-guessing ourselves,' continued Sponsorship. 'I believe that if we do that, however, we will not be serving the best interests of this organization that pays our salaries. After all,' he said pointing around the room, 'we are the leadership of this company.'

Vision began pacing. As if on cue, Sponsorship acknowledged Vision and stated, 'Vision has brought some needs of the organization to my attention over the past couple of weeks. She has been busy analyzing the market, our competitors and our effectiveness. One of the opportunities she has brought to my attention is our time-to-market history compared to our competitors. Over the last year or two, we have fallen behind and I am convinced that we must improve in that area to remain competitive.' She paused for a moment glancing around the room and then said, 'For us to regain our competitive edge I'm convinced that we need a big change.'

Just then the door opened, and a gigantic figure entered the room. The Change had to be one of the biggest ones any of them had ever seen. Even PECS looked diminutive compared to this big change. Wide eyes, silence and open mouths characterized the response. Communication noted the large 'IT' on Big Change's shirt and wondered what it was supposed to mean. Sponsorship resumed his introduction, 'Ladies and gentlemen, this is Big Change. I suspect that everyone recognizes him as information technology.' Sponsorship noticed that Communication blushed for some unknown reason.

Culture had not had any further encounters with Fear since they spoke in the hospital several days ago. Suddenly she noticed him pacing in the back of the room. Their eyes met and he waved and offered a knowing smile that made her uncomfortable. She wondered if anyone else saw Fear. Sponsorship continued, 'Our information technology is simply dated and that is a major component affecting our time-to-market, not to mention a number of other areas that diminish our competitiveness. Big Change is here today just for introductions. He will join us full-time in four weeks. You need to understand my position on this. I am convinced we must get Big Change integrated into our operations.' He turned to Commitment and as if reading from a cue card (although the words did not lack passion), Commitment began to discuss what would need to happen over the next four weeks to prepare the organization for Big Change.

Commitment shared the plan to follow the DISCUSS model which was created after the last failed change attempt was put to rest. Sometimes the best learning comes from evaluating what went wrong, and that was how the DISCUSS model came into existence. Commitment shared the seven steps of the DISCUSS model which seemed to greatly resonate with the leaders, as they listened closely with heads nodding at each important step.

- **D:** First we must clearly **define the change**. People will not support what they do not understand. Our employees deserve a crystal-clear answer to three questions: What is changing? Why is it changing? And how will it affect me?
- **I:** Next, we will **implement in phases.** Trying to implement everything at once is a recipe for confusion and chaos. We will build momentum with a clear plan and one step at a time.

- **S:** Although we have the leadership team in this room, we will expand our reach and **seek advocates and feedback** from employees across the organization to help ensure the change is a success. This will include forming pilot groups and identifying change champions across all departments. We will create anonymous channels for honest feedback (surveys, suggestion boxes and digital forms) to continuously take our change temperature.
- **C:** We must **communicate continuously**. Our communication strategy must be well embedded into our culture. We will communicate early, often, and through as many channels as required to reach all employees.
- **U:** We will **upskill** since new changes often require new skills. We will invest early and often in upskilling our people, so no one is left behind.
- **S:** We will **stay the course.** Energy will be high in the beginning, but then obstacles will appear, and the reality becomes more challenging. As leaders, we will model resiliency and strive to remain positive and keep the end goal top of mind.
- **S:** We will **share successes** throughout this entire journey. We will celebrate not just what we achieved, but how we have achieved it together. There is unity in community and we will work together to accomplish this change initiative.

Commitment held everyone's attention and the energy in the room grew in anticipation of this new plan for change success.

No one was paying attention to the large air duct over the refrigerator in the back corner of the room and when a 'metallic' sound came from that part of the room, everyone subconsciously assumed the noise came from the refrigerator. Mums had instinctively brought his hand to his mouth when his pen had fallen from his shirt pocket and landed on the floor of the air duct. After a deliberate pause, Mums peeked back out of the ventilation cover and was relieved to see no one was looking in his direction. Well, no one except perhaps Fear. Mums thought he saw Fear's eyes rest on the ventilator cover momentarily, but then Fear looked away. Mums had been there the whole time and had heard everything. He too had been awestruck by the Big Change's size. And they planned on him starting here in just four weeks. This was huge news. He smiled as he envisioned the look of pleasure on Resistance's face when he would tell him all he had heard in this meeting. Carefully, Mums turned in the tight quarters of the air duct and began to make his way back to Resistance and the Family.

Dear Diary,

It was interesting watching the reactions of everyone in the room today when this new change was announced. As we learned from our recent failure, any type of change comes with a responsibility that starts with the leadership.

After our meeting today, I wrote down the steps of the DISCUSS model introduced by Commitment. These are important actions that will help guide future change success. I have created additional clarification for the DISCUSS model to provide context for our team. Consistency and a unified approach are important for every change initiative.

The DISCUSS Model:

D: Define the Change
I: Implement in Phases
S: Seek Advocates and Feedback
C: Communicate Continuously
U: Upskill… Always
S: Stay the Course
S: Share Successes

D: Define the Change

- Although this may sound simple, there are many pieces to defining the change. It begins with gaining clarity about the whats of the change: What is the change, what is the reason for the change, what will improve as a result of the change, what is driving the change, and what will happen if we do not change?
- A second part of defining change is clarifying how. How will we implement this change? How will we gain support inside the organization? How will we roll this change out to the masses? How will we communicate this change?
- The third key word for defining change is who. Although it is likely that some changes will impact everyone, it is also important that individual responsibilities are identified to keep momentum moving forward. As the old saying goes, if everyone is in charge, no one is in charge. Who specifically will own various responsibilities of implementing this change? Who will hold individuals accountable for their role in this process? Who needs to be involved from across the organization? Who are our key stakeholders at the various levels?

I: Implement in Phases

Dividing a big change into smaller projects or phases has many benefits. With many changes, the change landscape often shifts, so this allows those in charge to make adjustments where necessary and move to the next phase.

This also allows the organization to clearly see the change progress being made. Implementing a big change can be a daunting task, so project management tools are essential to manage the process and identify wins along the way. Also, anytime we can uncomplicate the process and create a clear vision of what is next is helpful for all involved.

S: Seek Advocates and Feedback

When implementing a big change, some leaders default to making all the decisions themselves. This is not a winning strategy for big change. In order to obtain greater buy-in, take some time to consider who are key users or stakeholders across the organization who could provide valuable feedback and insight.

Many times, these individuals are formal or informal leaders across the organization who have tremendous influence with their peers. These individuals are often future leaders of the organization. Involve them. Ask for their ideas, insight and feedback. Ask for their support as they talk with other employees across the organization about this big change.

C: Communicate Continuously

Often, big changes begin with a flurry of meetings, activity and energy, but over time, the pace of the day job can sometimes creep in and take priority. This is why communication with the big change champions and communication with the entire organization about progress made are very important. These communications help keep individuals motivated and interested in the big change progress.

What are examples of different types of communications that could be used to keep interest focused on the big change? Here are a few but there are many more, such as:

1) Senior leader comments in meetings or newsletters
2) Town Hall meetings

3) Quarterly change project update meetings—virtual or in-person
4) Newsletters
5) Department meetings
6) Success or special recognition

The important thing to remember is that continuous communication is vital to the success of the project.

U: Upskill… Always

Most changes are going to require new processes, policies, technology, systems, approaches and tools, and this is going to require a focus on training, development and providing resources to help employees develop the skills needed to be ready for these new changes. This should not be an afterthought. Developing the skills for new technologies is an important part of the big change discussion.

Upskilling conversations at the beginning of the change initiation process should include the following:

- What new skills will be needed for this new change?
- Do we currently have these skills in-house, or do we need to develop these skills through training, coaching, on-demand programs, workshops, AI programs, webinars or learning from experts?
- How will we upskill our employees? When will we do this? Who will organize this training?

S: Stay the Course

No matter the change, there will be times when the journey seems to drag on and on, or the energy from the team starts to fizzle. It's OK! This is normal! When this happens, it may be time to shake things up, gather the group together for some networking, teambuilding, and resource wrangling. Resource wrangling is when someone has hit a wall with a particular part of their project and needs some ideas, feedback, suggestions or help to get back on track.

The important thing to remember is to stay the course. By this time, much has been accomplished, and we are getting closer to the finish line. Remember that it is OK to ask for assistance when working on projects. Each person's contribution is very important! It will most likely impact our culture for years to come.

S: Share Successes

As part of this team meeting to regroup, refresh and reenergize, please remember to share your success stories along the way. It is important to share these wins and successes not only with each other but also with others inside the organization so they can see the finish line too.

Contract on Big Change

People don't resist change. They resist being changed!

—Peter Senge

Day 8

Resistance ordered 'The Hit'.

It was evening now. Mums had come to Resistance with information about the Big Change that was coming. Mums had been surprised at Resistance's reaction. He thought Resistance would be pleased with the news. On the contrary, Resistance got angry when Mums told him about Big Change. The rage, however, was not directed at Mums. That was not Resistance's style, and he quickly made it clear to Mums that he appreciated how he had gained the information and relayed it so quickly. The source of the anger was the timing and magnitude of the change. Resistance knew that such a big change in the wake of the recent death of Change could be just too much for the organization to handle. On the other hand and depending on the leadership's response to Change's murder, the imminent arrival of Big Change so soon could feasibly be the springboard to propel ACME to a highly successful future. Resistance could not allow that to happen and so he called an emergency meeting of the Family.

With his Family assembled, including Fear this time, Resistance had Mums relate the information he had learned earlier in the day about Big Change. When Mums had finished,

Resistance looked at Fear and asked, 'What do you think?' Fear had given the 'free agent' speech to Resistance several years ago and although Resistance could not say he fully understood the implications of this, he had now come to understand that somehow when he asked Fear a question or for advice, it was more a matter of introspection versus receiving an outside opinion.

Fear replied simply, 'It's a defining moment.'

Looking directly at Fear, Resistance acknowledged agreement with a nodding of the head and then he turned to the Family. He began pacing around the table. He picked up a baseball bat and began slapping it rhythmically into his open palm and he said, 'I want Big Change dead. You hear me? Dead! Not injured. Not in the hospital ICU. Dead and buried. Do I make myself clear?' The family members nodded that he had made himself clear. Resistance had a flip chart at the front of the room. He walked up to it and removed the blank page on top to reveal:

OVERWHELM
Culture Shock Disbelief Denial 'Not Again!' ***Feels Like Too Much!***

He pointed at the top of the chart with his metal pointer. 'First,' he pronounced with authority, 'we will overwhelm them.' He looked around the room and then added, 'In case you don't know who "them" refers to, I am talking about the line employees—the ones who do the real work here.' The audience nodded in understanding. We will get them asking and thinking about these overwhelm questions. He turned the page and read the bullet points.

- What is happening? How can this happen again?
- We just went through a big change. Did we not learn how hard it is to implement change?
- What do they want from us? I'm going to ignore it and hope it goes away.
- Who else is swamped? I can't think about this right now; I'm too busy.
- Why can't they just leave things alone? Everytime we get comfortable with our work process, they change things up and disrupt the process. This is too much! It is overwhelming.

'We will use our Resistance tools and give them a shock!' Resistance added emphatically. 'A Culture Shock. We will have them reeling.' Looking at Psychs, he said, 'We will put them in denial and disbelief.' To Mums he said, 'We will have them crying "Oh no. Not again, It's too much!"'

Resistance turned the flip-chart page saying, 'And that's when some of our core members will do their work to get the employees to outright oppose Big Change. Fear, Chaos and Confusion.' His voice grew louder, 'this is where you shall shine!'

Enter Resistance Family Fear Confusion Chaos Frustration Anger ***Feels Like Us Against Them!***
OPPOSE

We will get the employees engaged in these resistant thoughts and behaviors. Again, he turned the page and read the bullet points, which said the following:

- The last Change failed, and this one will fail too. I won't be a part of it.
- Negative gossip: Did you hear that the only reason we are moving forward with this change is so that the IT department can get a raise?
- This will never work. Why doesn't leadership ever learn from their mistakes? When will they ever learn?
- Our entire department is against this plan. No one supports it. Good luck getting people on board.
- I'm out of here if they make us move forward with this change. Who's coming with me?

When he finished the bullet points, he walked around the room slowly with his bat in his hand. Finally, he said, 'Overwhelm and oppose! Do you get it? Overwhelm and oppose!' The members of the Family began to chant it.

When the chanting died out, Axe, who did not want to be left out, stood up and said, 'I can take Big Change out. I don't care how big he is.' Immediately the gang began chattering to one another. Resistance only heard the odd words here and there; kill, poison, delay, sabotage—but none of it made sense to him. Both Chaos and Confusion were smiling. He put both hands up and the chatter ceased.

He said, 'Look, no heroes on this one. We have to work together as a team.' Axe appeared to be brooding. Resistance continued, 'Axe, I am not angry at you. In fact, I applaud the passion. I just want to make sure we channel that passion into a collective action plan that ensures our success. I've ordered dinner to be delivered. I'm pretty sure we are going to need to work around the clock for a while. Anyone have issues with that?' There were no issues with anyone staying, until he got to Fear. Fear shrugged his shoulders, and Resistance interpreted the gesture as a nonverbal 'it's outside my control.'

He asked Fear to step outside for a minute. Now in the hall, Resistance spoke, 'Look, I need you on this one.'

Fear replied, 'Haven't I been there when you needed me in the past?'

A look of reminiscence came over Resistance's face. 'We grew up together, we're practically family. Remember in grade school when we would take the lunch money from the other kids?' Fear smiled. Resistance continued, 'Yes, I have pretty much been able to depend on you in the past but I have to tell you that in the last couple of years or so you have worried me a few times.' Resistance could not detect any emotion from Fear. 'This Big Change is among the most intensive we've come up against and unless we have Fear at 100 per cent, I'm not sure we can prevent the integration.'

There was a momentary pause. Fear wanted to ensure Resistance was finished. With great patience, he stated, 'I am a free agent. We've had that discussion. So you understand that you're not the only one who wants or needs me. Consequently, I will not guarantee that I will be visible here all night long. But do not mistake my visibility for my presence. I do not question your ways of getting things done and I ask you not to question mine. I heard your directive. You do not want Big Change to survive.'

Resistance rubbed his eyes. Was Fear fading? Resistance could see right through him. Fear's last sentence before disappearing was, 'You do not want Big Change to survive but a lot of people here do.' He was gone, and Resistance began to understand about feeling Fear's presence even though he couldn't see him.

Dear Diary,

One thing I often wonder about is how far will Resistance go to sabotage a big change? Over the years, I have witnessed many forms of resistance, from intentional indifference to full-scale initiatives to stop change from launching and succeeding. I can feel a similar energy that is surrounding this Big Change, and although I have not heard specific plans of resistance, I feel a resistance storm is brewing, and like any weather phenomenon, all the components are coming together for the perfect storm.

Wouldn't it be wonderful if all changes were welcomed with open minds, and a willingness to learn, adapt and grow? It may be a lovely scenario, but chances are, there will always be some form of what feels like pushback when new changes are announced and that is not a bad thing.

I think it all depends on what the pushback is and how it is presented. For example, when some changes are announced, employees, for example, may have a lot of questions and this can be a good thing. In fact, it is very important to obtain the employee viewpoint upfront and listen to their ideas before announcing and launching a change initiative. Questions employees may ask are: What is driving this change at this time? When is this going to take place? What exactly will change? How will things be different in our department? What is my role in this change? These are great questions because they help leadership make sure all details have been considered prior to implementation.

The part of resistance that worries me the most is the behind-the-scenes resistance. Some of my biggest surprises in my role have come from individuals who have professed their support for change, but unfortunately their behaviors and words behind the scenes created a much different picture about their actual non-support. I have often wondered what happened to turn some of our most loyal champions into members of the Resistance Family.

- Did we make mistakes on previous change initiatives that have eroded the trust individuals have in our leadership team?
- Were there moments when we didn't behave in alignment with our values?
- Do we have some of the leaders on board, but not all of them, and therefore it seems like we are sending out mixed messages?
- Do we really know how many leaders actually support this new initiative or do we have a lot of people sitting on the fence and taking a wait-and-see approach? We need them to be active members on the Big Change team.
- Have we misjudged the influence of the Resistance Family? Are there more resistors than we know?

These are some of the questions that are keeping me up at night. I just have a sinking feeling that the resistance storm is taking a turn for the worse and we just don't know where it will hit.

I think I'm going to pay closer attention to what is happening around me. I have been observing behaviors and listening to concerns, but I will be more intentional. Here are some actions I will initiate starting tomorrow.

- I will set up one-on-one conversations with leaders and members of our executive team so I can ask questions and find out how people are feeling. For those who may have hesitations or concerns, I will listen carefully to them, hear their concerns, and provide information and resources to help clear up any confusion. In addition to the one-on-one meetings, I'll also implement quick culture chats with employees—five-minute chats in the breakroom, mailroom and other common spaces to take the temperature of how people are really feeling.

- I also know some of our leaders are very positive about this change and have taken on more responsibility to help with this initiative. I also want to thank them for their support and energy for this new change. I don't think we have done a good-enough job thanking our employees and leaders for their change efforts. All of this takes extra time, effort, learning new skills and defining new processes on top of the day job.
- I will also connect with key organizational influencers/employees and ask for their feedback about Big Change. If they are unhappy, they have the ability to influence several others to join their thinking. This could be a big setback. But if they see value in the big change, and are on board with the improvements it will bring, this could help us tremendously with our organizational buy-in.
- I will also recommend that we increase the communication frequency to reach people in a variety of different ways. We need to be clear on our messaging and the story/vision of this big change. We need to keep it simple, not over-complicate the messaging, but people need to hear why this is so important, and why now.

Balancing Values

Open your arms to change, but don't let go of your values.

—Dalai Lama

Day 12

The doctor had been right when he had stated this about Culture: 'She's going to live but she'll never be the same.' Communication had noted that she did not seem to have as much trouble hearing and understanding Culture. The volume of her speech had normalized—no episodes or whispering or screaming—and Communication believed that somehow the phenomenon went deeper than volubility. Performance noted that Culture was just around more. In the past she would have labeled her as aloof, but over the past few weeks, she assessed her to be accessible and engaged in what was going on in the organization.

Although oblivious to the fact that her team members were viewing her differently, Culture was tuned in to how she was seeing herself. The series of events—Change's death, her shock, her conversation with Fear and the introduction of Big Change—had given her a reason to pause and reflect. In the past, she had seen the organization's success as a natural outcome of her own success. But that was over 25 years ago. It had taken her some time back then to instill the basic assumptions and beliefs about how the organization should work. Once the assumptions and beliefs were embedded, Culture had relied on tradition to pass the baton from employee to employee. Gradually, her need to be visible in the organization diminished. That's not to say that she abandoned the organization by any means. She was there every day. If nothing else, Culture had a strong work ethic. It was just not necessary for the employees to see her routinely. Granted, her visible presence increased when a new leader came on board. She felt compelled to personally ensure that leaders of high ranking in the organization were informed first-hand of the groundwork she had laid. A couple of CEOs over the years had actually tried to reframe the basic assumptions and beliefs under a banner of 'Progress' or 'Times Have Changed', but she dismissed their assertions to naivety and youth and in the end, they were no longer there, and she was. Looking back, she questioned herself as to whether she had truly had the best interest of the organization at heart.

Culture reflected back on entries in her diary on the values she helped to conceive, birth and nurture in the organization, and considered their relevancy for the future.

Dear Diary,

The Values, in and of themselves, are both relevant and respectable. The problem is that of balance. By relying on tradition for the transfer of Values, the organization had migrated to extremes with these Values in an attempt to respond to the evolving market and other pressures. Those extremes presented some challenges for the organization.

- **Very efficient:** With such an intense focus on efficiency, the organization perhaps failed to see the opportunity cost of not investing in needed resources and spending money on training and equipment to allow them to remain competitive.

- **A customer focus:** The organization never really lost sight of the 'paying' customer, those that purchased their products, but they had strayed from consistently recognizing one another—leaders, managers and staff as customers. Years ago, someone had defined the customer as 'the next person in the process' and while they had once practiced this philosophy, today it was a rare occurrence.
- **Lots of teamwork:** Perhaps this was the Value that the organization had taken to the most extreme, particularly at the leadership and management level where they talked about teamwork but actually operated in silos. If we are focused on teamwork, why are we rewarding individual performance and not team performance?
- **Understanding:** Listening and understanding had been displaced by hidden agendas—discourse and verbosity—that became a surrogate prop for informed decision-making.
- **Excellence:** Excellence had been replaced by compromise. The products were still good, still acceptable, but the number of defects, time to market and other indicators had put the organization in the ill-favored category of average.

I will not allow this train of thought to suppress my mood. On the contrary, Sponsorship's words came back to me: 'We could all spend a lot of time looking back and second-guessing ourselves. I believe if we do that, we will not be serving the best interests of this organization.'

Dear Diary,

Since the meeting where Big Change was introduced, I have spent a lot of time with Sponsorship. He has communicated to me that he was depending on me to set the tone to integrate Big Change and had even asked me to be his partner in this initiative.

Yes, we can depend on our values as a foundation to integrate Big Change. We just have to bring them back into balance and somehow make them actionable for our people. I, Culture, must support this Big Change, and I must keep an eye on this Resistance Family.

When I was in the hospital, I overheard the doctor talking with the nurse. Although I was in an altered level of consciousness, I heard, 'she's going to live but she'll never be the same.' He was right. I am going to live and I'm not going to be the same. I am going to be better.

Confusion and Chaos Meet the Employees

Every great change is preceded by chaos.

—Deepak Chopra

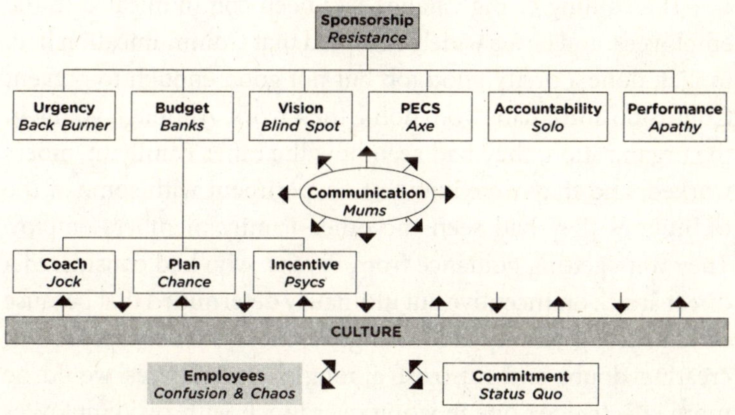

Day 16

Two weeks had passed since Big Change's introduction to the leadership and two more weeks were left before he would begin his formal orientation at ACME organization. Both sides, the Leadership/Management Team and the Resistance Family, had been very busy. Sponsorship and Culture had planned for and scheduled a two-day meeting with a primary objective of developing an action plan to integrate Big Change. The Resistance Family met nightly, developing their strategy to kill Big Change. Some of the most interesting meetings had already taken place, mostly in private.

Confusion and Chaos were having a blast. Their main target was the employees and for them it was like being on spring break. They met with the employees, sometimes one-on-one but more commonly in groups of two or three. They could be found having lunch with a few folks from the same department or in the break room, or even after hours as long as they were back in time for the Family meetings.

The coming of Big Change had been communicated to the employees, and it was widely accepted that Communication had, in fact, done a pretty good job but not good enough to prevent Confusion and Chaos from doing their work. Although young in the organization, they had seen how the other Family members worked, and they were known to experiment with some of the techniques they had seen the other Family members employ. They were getting guidance from Psychs, who had considered a direct attack on Incentive but ultimately determined that because of her strong affinity for Change, a more subtle approach of creating doubt and mistrust among the employees would be more effective. At one meeting over lunch with two employees from the purchasing department, they used these techniques they learnt from Psychs.

Paula said to Barry, 'Do you really think this Big Change is going to work here?'

Barry responded after taking a drink from his soda, 'Maybe. I mean Communication seemed positive about it and you and I both know that the current information system we have is archaic.'

Confusion whispered to Paula, 'It might be a bit archaic, but it works. You know it works. Why do we need Change? What's really wrong with how things are now? What's really in it for you anyway? How long will it take you to learn this new system? And even when you have learned it, how do you really know it will work as well for you as the current system?'

At the same time Chaos had Barry's ear. He said, 'You don't have time to spend in training on this new system. Do you think your manager is going to relieve you of your other responsibilities? The answer is no. She will expect the same level of output from you and for you to learn this system.'

Barry said, 'I wish they would just leave us alone. They could have at least asked for our opinion about the system. Maybe it won't happen. Sometimes they make these big announcements and then nothing happens.'

Paula responded, 'I bet they haven't even thought about all the interfaces this new system will need. A friend of mine works for a company that introduced a new, large IT system over two years ago and they still haven't worked out all the bugs.'

Knowing their work was finished with these two employees, Confusion and Chaos smiled at one another and left to find other employees that they had not visited yet.

None of them noticed Culture, who was sitting at the table right next to them. She wrote:

Dear Diary,

Confusion and Chaos can be expected with such a large Change, and they know exactly who to target—our employees. But can we keep them out?

I must discuss with Communication. We certainly can do a much better job of surfacing and addressing our employees' concerns, not only at the announcement phase but also throughout the implementation. Without consistent and accurate information, our employees are susceptible to the whims of Confusion and Chaos.

It doesn't take much to plant a seed of doubt.

A few months ago, I was enjoying coffee on my front porch overlooking a farmer's field in the distance. It was early in the morning and the farmer had already been hard at work for hours. As I reflect on that morning, observing the farmer and thinking about our current situation with Confusion and Chaos, some obvious connections come to mind.

The power of a seed. It starts so small and is packed with so much potential. With a new seed/planting comes the hope of a successful crop. In order for the seed to grow, there are many things that need to happen to nurture the seed. The farmer's objective is to protect that seed and remove obstacles that threaten to harm it. Here are other parallels I see with the farmer and implementing Big Change to reduce Chaos and Confusion:

- **Preparation of the soil:** Farmers use science and generations of wisdom to make sure the soil is adequately prepared and ready for the next crop. Similarly for Big Change, preparation is vital. Clarity and communication are key. Leadership must be informed, on board, and ready to champion the change. Big Change is not just implemented by leadership, so preparing the employees for what is coming, why it is important, what will change going forward, and how will this impact them is extremely important.
- **Control the controllables:** Certainly, in farming the weather can be a difficult subject, but over the

years, many practices have been implemented to be strategic and plant the right crop at the right time—to deal with environmental issues. For change, controlling the controllables means completing the due diligence to strategize the plan for this Big Change. It means creating a project plan that lists the key action items, assigns accountability and due dates, and addresses dependencies and contingencies. Too many organizations rush into a big change with a flurry of urgency, without thinking through all the many 'what ifs' and potential impacts to various parts of the business. It is fair to assume that we may never anticipate every nuance to a change, but we must be strategic, plan ahead and control the controllables.

- **Pest control:** Farmers take a strong stance against insects and animals who want to devour their crops during every stage of the growing cycle. These pests might consist of beetles, worms, ants, spiders, mice, rats and many more. For this reason, farmers check fields regularly. Farming, like leadership, is never 'once and done'. While in the fields, they look for damage and treat problem areas promptly with a variety of approaches. For an infestation, farmers act quickly.

Confusion and Chaos can have a similar destructive impact on the success of Big Change, or even small change. Confusion and Chaos seek to undermine, derail, confuse, sabotage, weaken and impede efforts to implement new change.

It is amazing that these seeds of doubt they plant can be started with a simple question, an inaccurate statement about the organization's intent, or planting a seed of a fear that was not in existence seconds before the conversation.

Confusion and Chaos like company. Just like the farmer's field of insects, they believe the more the merrier!

For this reason, our leaders need to talk with their employees regularly. They will need to provide reassurance, accurate information, and details to keep Confusion and Chaos at bay. Be honest. Be Authentic. Secrets, half-truths, spin language and limited communication can all have a negative impact on the success of Big Change.

We need to make sure we have our eyes and ears wide open to observe and listen for signs that Confusion and Chaos have been planting seeds of doubt and destruction.

The Budget Meeting

People don't buy what you do; they buy why you do it.

—Simon Sinek

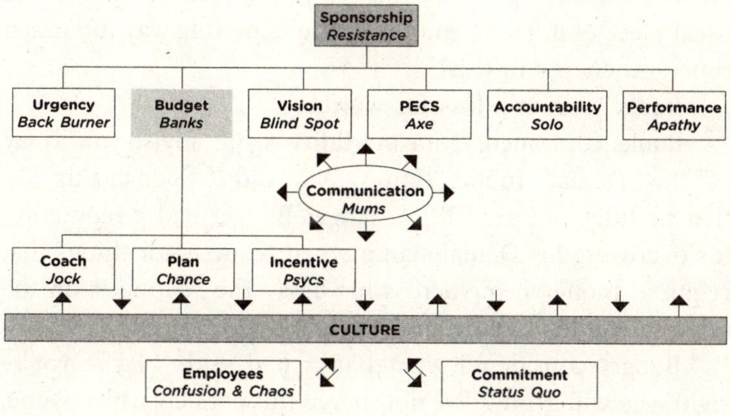

Day 17

A few days earlier, Banks had showed up in Budget's office. It was early in the evening and Budget was working on the financing plan for the big change. Banks was dressed as he had been in the initial Family meeting: expensive tailored suit, shoes and jewelry. Budget's first impression of Banks was that he looked like a high-rolling drug dealer.

Budget said, 'Can I help you? How did you get in here?'

Without any sign of unease, Banks took a chair across the desk from Budget and replied, 'It's 7:00 p.m. Your assistant is gone, and I'm really here to help you.'

Budget stared at him for a few moments and stated, 'Who are you and what makes you think I need your help?'

Banks reclined in the chair a bit, put his feet on the desk and pulled an expensive cigar from his breast pocket. Budget was about to say, 'I don't allow smoking in here.' Banks, as if anticipating the statement, said, 'I never light them up. Just chew on them a bit.' He went on. 'Look, I know what's going on with Big Change and I can see you are wrestling with the fiscal piece of it. Don't you think you're putting way too much time and energy in this?'

Budget was at a loss for words.

Banks continued, 'I mean, didn't Agent advise you to lay off the "Denial" rubber stamp? And didn't Sponsorship say that he fully endorsed Big Change? Budget had a reputation for overusing his Denial stamp when requests for things that required money came across his desk. The writing is on the wall, so why dive into the details?'

Budget considered what Banks had said. 'Maybe you're right,' she said firmly. 'I've not shared this publicly with anyone, but I do feel a level of responsibility for the last Change's death.' She was surprised at herself for sharing such intimate thought with a perfect stranger but felt compelled to expunge herself. 'This conversation will stay in this room?' she asked seriously.

'Oh, absolutely,' he replied. 'Mum's the word.' He chuckled to himself, making a mental note to not to forget to tell Mums about his little play on words later.

Uncharacteristically, Budget reached up and pulled the pin from her bun letting her hair flow down past her shoulders. She said, 'I really want Big Change to be successful. I've hardly slept since the other Change died. I know he was right about some of the things he said. It is so hard to let go though. I have taken my responsibilities here very seriously for many years.'

'As you should. As you should!' said Banks emphatically. 'And I bet you've not taken a real vacation since you've been here.' She nodded in agreement. Banks knew he was drawing her in. 'Now's the time,' he said. 'You've virtually been given the license to open up the purse strings, the way I see it. Look at the purchase order requests on your desk. Big Change is not the only area that needs people, equipment and training. If you ask me, it's time to loosen up. Get out the "Approved" rubber stamp, dust off the cobwebs and use it.'

Thoughtfully, Budget said, 'You know, you may be right.'

Getting up to leave, Banks smiled and said, 'Of course I'm right. Just common sense, isn't it?' As he neared the door, Budget said, 'But you never told me who you are. How can I contact you if I need to?'

'Not to worry. I'll be around.' He closed the door and was gone.

Budget could normally see Culture easily. One could say they had become 'tight' over the years. Yet, Budget was unaware of Culture's presence during this ad hoc and very interesting meeting. Once the stranger was gone, Budget left her office. Culture stayed and reflected on what she had witnessed. She wrote:

Dear Diary,

We must exert some control over Budget. I've known her for years and I believe she gets a bad rap. She truly has the organization's best interest at heart. Perhaps she was overzealous with her denial stamp with the last Change. It is difficult to say. It is possible that she actually saved the organization a lot of money and heartache by being realistic about our low commitment to that change. But now, this character is actually encouraging her to swing to the other end of the pendulum.

Balance, that is what we must have with our Budget… balance. I must work on getting Plan out of the clouds and to work closely with Budget. Infrastructure must be involved as well.

I will reintroduce Budget to ROI (short for Return on Investment). It is not that our Budget does not know ROI. He certainly comes up now and then. But with this Big Change, we must lean on him to help both the leadership and employees understand what we can expect in return for our allocation of resources toward this change. He will provide reasonable estimates for how this Change will affect our income and our expenses. He will give us his forecast for both the short-term and long-term effects of this change. These predictions will help us set goals so we can track our progress. There are some who see ROI as black and white, debits and credits, if you will. But our ROI has a human side too. He not only considers the financial implications, he is also very aware of the potential human consequences in a big change like this one. He will remind Budget that we must be thoughtful when we pull our employees for training, that there is still their day job to be done, and we must make a reasonable accommodation for that. He will remind Budget that we are fond of saying here at ACME Organization that 'people are our greatest asset' and that Big Change is an opportunity to demonstrate that.

With ROI by Budget's side and with Communication's guidance, we will provide an in-depth and honest accounting of the fiscal and human resources it will take to make this Big Change successful. We owe that to ourselves, our employees and our investors.

Vision and Self-Reflection

Culture change becomes embedded when people personalize the vision and live in their daily activities.

—Harry Paul, *FISH!*

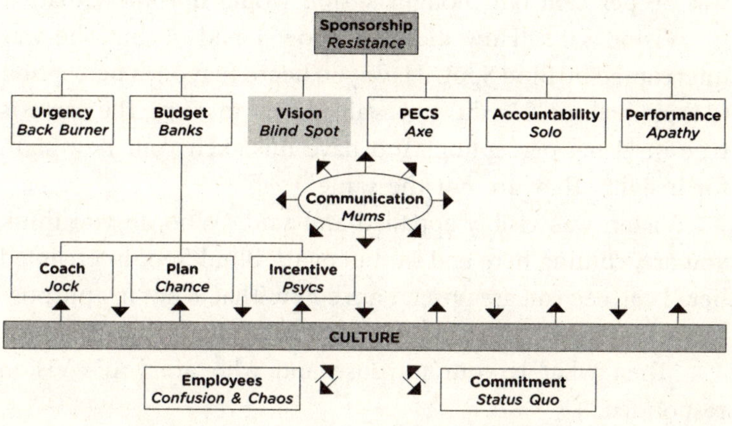

Day 18

The previous Monday, Vision had a private meeting of her own. ACME organization was a one-story building and Blind Spot found Vision early in the morning on the roof looking through her telescope. Vision nearly jumped out of her skin when Blind Spot tapped her on the shoulder. Her alarm was intensified when she turned to see the pirate-looking character standing before her. Blind Spot was dressed in solid black. His black hair and beard were both unkempt and the one eye not covered by a patch had a dark circle under it, leading Vision to believe sleep had abandoned this man. Vision actually found herself averting her eyes to the man's side, half-expecting to find a sword.

'I'm sorry,' Vision offered. 'But you startled me.'

Without introduction, Blind Spot said, 'You know Lasik surgery is only effective in achieving and maintaining 20/20 vision 50 per cent of the time.' He knew that the real statistic was 86 per cent but thought Vision would not know that.

Vision said, 'How did you know I had—,' but she was interrupted by Bind Spot. 'Have you heard that one's perception is their reality?' He did not wait for an answer. 'The same is true in visual perception. You have mistaken your new sight for insight. They are not the same.'

Vision was visibly appalled and said, 'Who do you think you are, coming here and—,' but again Blind Spot interrupted her. 'I can see you are upset. I am sorry. That is not my purpose for being here.'

'Then what is your purpose and who are you?' Vision responded.

'My name—or who I am—is not important,' responded Blind Spot. 'Suffice it to say I probably know and understand you better than anyone. Think now. This is not the first time you've seen me.'

Vision became pensive. She closed her eyes and searched. From somewhere deep in her subconscious, she found it. Vision was known for standing at the window and staring out. She was sure that her peers believed she was always looking outward. After all, that was her job. And most of the time that is exactly what she did. Every now and then, however, she was actually looking at herself, her reflection in the window. This self-reflection was not an act of egotism but one of introspection. In her mind, she was always looking out for others, for the organization. She needed these rare moments of introspection as a sanity check. How could she have forgotten these incidents though? They came back to her as if a vague dream. She knew there was more to it that she would never recall, but what she did remember was that a few times when she was looking at her reflection in the window, another reflection, besides her own, stood staring at her for a fleeting moment. It was him! The same man on the roof was him. She opened her eyes.

Blind Spot knew from Vision's expression that she was now aware.

With an air of resignation, Vision asked, 'What do you want?'

'I just want you to see what I see.'

'And that is?'

Blind spot began. 'You recently had a murder here. Change. I might suggest that you had some complicity in that. I am not suggesting that we, I mean you, were totally responsible but that I agree with Agent's assessment. There was a collective culpability. My question to you is this. In the wake of such a recent failure, as it related to Change and even with your eye surgery, do you really believe you can trust your sight, your perception, to recommend such a big change so soon?'

Blind Spot could tell Vision was weighing her words carefully. He started to say more but determined it prudent to stop there.

When Vision finally pulled herself out of her deep thoughts, she looked up. The man was gone. She turned and took a few steps back toward the telescope. For some unknown reason she changed her mind and left the roof.

Culture remained on the roof to contemplate this unusual meeting. She too was a bit surprised to see this…this Blind Spot. The organization's Vision had surely transformed since the death of the last Change, and Culture assessed it to be a very positive transformation. She wrote:

Dear Diary,

I am confident that Vision's guidance has led us to this right new Change, and yet this Blind Spot, he concerns me. What was it he said? 'You have mistaken your new sight for insight. They are not the same.' A good Vision will paint a clear picture of the future state and how it relates to Change. A great Vision will paint a clear picture of the future state and show how the employees fit into the picture. This last piece is what we have been missing. I must see Vision right away. As I prepare for this meeting, I am reminded how important Vision's role is to the success of Big Change. Vision has a responsibility to guide us into the future, but Vision must also stay cognizant of lessons learned from the past to keep us from repeating our mistakes. These Blind Spots may remain invisible unless they are spotted and addressed. The challenge is that when they remain invisible, they can cause significant disruption without being detected.

This is why Vision must operate with a 360-degree magnifying lens. Vision helps us forecast our future, learn from the past; it sets the foundation for our strategic planning, and must also be ready to adjust when the reality of our current state calls for flexibility. Industry changes, lightning-speed advances in technology, and workplace environment dynamics are constantly shifting, and Vision must be ready to assess, adopt and implement new strategies when needed. Gone are the days of the 'cast in stone' five-year vision statements.

When I meet with Vision, I will remind her that her values should include:

- Driving the organization into the future with a compelling vision, but also helping ACME recognize what is needed in our current state.
- Remembering lessons learned from the past.
- Uncovering blind spots. Blind spots may exist within our leadership team, our strategy design, our implementation process, or within me, our environment/Culture. Getting input from others is vitally important because many times our blind spots can remain invisible to us. What do others see that we are missing?
- Inspiring individuals and helping them recognize that they are vital in our Change process. It is not accurate just to say that we want the employees to be involved. The truth is that we must have our employees involved. They are the engine that makes our organization not only exist but thrive.
- Providing a clear and compelling vision that will unite our employees in a common purpose. Vision's influence on me, Culture, is critical. Vision has the remarkable ability to capture hearts and minds, which helps all of us see the future as though it already exists.
- A clear Vision reinforces the value that ongoing development and adopting a mindset of continuous process improvements are essential to Change success. These are important factors in our short- and long-term planning. The more leaders and employees take a

proactive role in their development, the more likely we can respond to Change with resilience and flexibility.

A few more thoughts that I will share with Vision and ask her questions about—in context of our past Changes—are:

- What assumptions do we default to that may not be accurate?
- Do we have trends of implementing action without doing our due diligence?
- Do we seek the advice of experts, or do we default to the opinions of a few?
- Do we use business tools to help us brainstorm, analyze, clarify and validate data, or are decisions made via discussions in team meetings?

- Vision must be entrenched in our organization. Are we doing all we can to keep Vision's messaging alive? This would include introducing Vision during onboarding, linking individual goals to our Vision, and keeping her front and center in team and department meetings.
- Success stories need to be validated and shared as part of the messaging. With this new Change, we should create short stories for key successes and tell those stories on repeat. What would our success stories be? There is great value in hearing about key successes through the spoken word.

The Consigliere: The Status Quo

One day everything will be well, that is our hope. Everything's fine today, that is our illusion.

—Voltaire

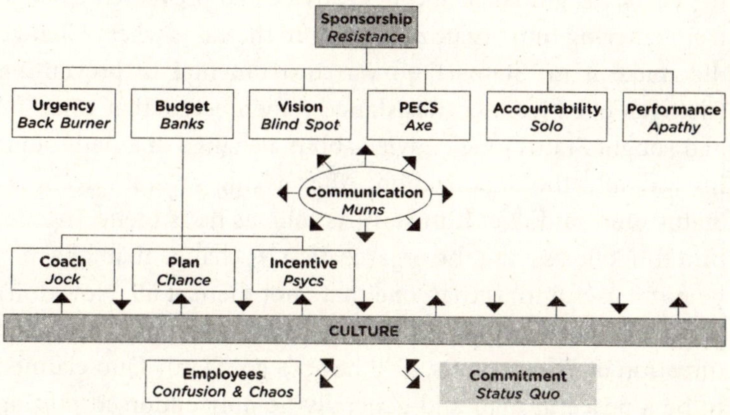

Day 19

Resistance had called the consigliere and asked to meet with him. He had been unavailable for the initial Family meeting where they had discussed Big Change, but was able to arrange the meeting a week later with a caveat. Resistance would have to come to him. For a number of reasons—confidentiality, protection and time constraints—the consigliere sent the message that he could meet but only on his own turf. This message did not surprise Resistance. He had needed to consult with the consigliere several times in his career and each time he had to go to him. Given the consigliere's position in the Administration, Resistance accepted this without question. His only concern was being away from ACME organization even for a few hours.

On the plane, Resistance closed his eyes, and his thoughts went to his history with the consigliere, known by the Family as Status Quo, a nickname bestowed upon him by the Boss. Over the years, his guidance and wise advice had prevented Change from entering into organizations, or in the cases where Change did make it in, Status Quo was instrumental in preventing Change's effectiveness. Resistance remembered that once he had sought Status Quo's advice about a change that had found his way into the organization. After asking several questions, Status Quo said, 'Let him stay. As long as he is ineffective, let him think he's saving the organization. A change that fails may be more useful to us than one that's not there at all. Now don't get me wrong. Keep an eye on him. If he starts moving in the direction of effectiveness, he'll have to go.' Status Quo claimed to be a peaceful man and generally he only endorsed putting out a contract when there was a big change. For dealing with smaller changes, he had other, more conservative means. He had a number of crews in organizations across the world that were similar to Resistance's. Status Quo had, in fact, designed the initial training sessions for these crew members. He would say, 'There's an art to subtlety. Don't shoot a mouse with a cannon. We want to stay off the radar screen, so use your basic tools first.'

Resistance then recalled that many years ago a member of

the Family openly disagreed with Status Quo. Status Quo told the member that they could talk privately after the meeting, but the member just would not let the issue go and continued to argue publicly. That was the last day anyone ever saw that member and since then no one, to Resistance's knowledge, had ever challenged the Status Quo openly again. Resistance opened his eyes as the plane touched down.

The meeting was scheduled for 1:00 p.m. at Rigionos, Status Quo's favorite restaurant. Resistance was fifteen minutes late and began offering his apologies as he approached the table. Status Quo stood and held his arms out to greet him. As Resistance provided the obligatory kiss on each cheek, Status Quo said, 'Look, no problem. Never on time. Planes, trains… who can trust them, eh? Sit, sit.'

As they both sat, Resistance noted that their table was well out of earshot of the other patrons. With a quick glance around the room, he eyed two men at two different tables that he deduced to be Status Quo's bodyguards.

'How have you been?' asked Resistance.

'Oh, the same. Always the same,' Status Quo said with a grin. They both chuckled.

After they had ordered their lunch, Status Quo said, 'My messenger said you sounded worried. How can I help you?'

Resistance communicated what had happened at ACME organization over the past seven to eight months including Change's initiatives, his death, Culture's shock, and the introduction of Big Change. 'I have to tell you,' said Resistance. 'This one really worries me.'

'Do you have a good team in place?' asked Status Quo.

'The best,' replied Resistance. 'I've worked with them for years.' He paused. 'The problem, I think, is Fear. I'm just not sure if Fear is with me or against me.'

Status Quo finished a sip of wine, wiped his mouth and leaned back in his chair. After a few moments he said with a knowing smile. 'Ah yes, Fear. I see.'

Resistance said, 'You know, maybe I'm overreacting. I mean, Fear has always been a good soldier. It's just that the last couple of years. Well, I'm starting to have doubts.'

Their lasagna came and they stopped the conversation. Once the waiter was gone, Status Quo tied his napkin around his neck and said, 'I suppose he's pulling that free agent stuff again?' Resistance nodded in agreement. Status Quo said, 'Eat. Eat. Nothing worse than cold lasagna.' They both ate in silence.

When he had finished his meal, Status Quo pulled the napkin from his neck, wiped his mouth and threw it on his plate. He pulled a cigar from his breast pocket and lit it. On cue, the waiter brought coffee. After a few drags on the cigar, he turned to Resistance and said, 'Fear has to be completely in or completely out. He cannot straddle the fence with Big Change. If it was up to me, I would have him iced.' He took another drag on the cigar and let out an exaggerated exhale. 'This is not the first time he has caused trouble. However, he saved the Boss's life about ten years ago and the Boss refuses to allow a contract on him. Let him know you've talked to me. Tell him I said it was all or nothing and that I said every decision has a consequence.' One of the bodyguards caught Status Quo's eye and he was tapping his watch. Status Quo took a sip of coffee, got up and put his coat on. He turned to Resistance and said, 'Keep Big Change out. Whatever you have to do, keep him out. With or without Fear.' He threw a hundred-dollar bill on the table and said as he was leaving, 'You've got to try the canola here. They're to die for.'

Culture could not be sure of the exact conversation between Resistance and Status Quo, but she had known many

Status Quos before. She knew that if Resistance was willing to risk a meeting with this high-ranking officer, she would need Communication to prepare the organization. She knew Resistance would come back armed with *status quo language* that would encourage the organization to hang on to the past. She also knew that Communication would need to ready the organization to counter that with *willing and upskilling language* that represented a desire to move on, not hold on. She drew a diagram on her diary and wrote:

Dear Diary,

Willing & Upskilling
Learn New Skills
Share Successes
Lots of Communication
Gaining Momentum
Feels Possible!
OPTIMIZE

Fear is a puzzle to me. Fear can keep ACME employees frozen in time, unable to take a single step forward, and afraid to move beyond the status quo. At the same time, Fear can also be a motivator to get unstuck, to move forward, and to proceed with speed and resilience. We must move forward and optimize this change! How will we know when we are stuck, or if we are willing to move forward and improve our skills?

The answers may be revealed in the language that we hear across the organization. Do we hear status quo language or willing and upskilling language? Here is what these two types of language might sound like:

Example 1

Status quo language: We have tried this before and it didn't work. Why bother trying it again? This is not a good use of our time. I was here when we tried something like this several years ago. All that work, and it wasn't even successful. What a waste of time and effort. This is the way we have always done it.

Willing and upskilling language: It's true. We may have tried a similar implementation before, but we have never tried it from where we are right now. There is no time like the present. Things are different now than they once were several years ago. Since then, we have had more experiences and successes, gained better business knowledge; we have learned from previous project implementations, we have better tools and we have acquired more wisdom.

So, today is a new day! In fact, because we have tried it before, if this solution is still relevant and the best path, this may be the perfect time to try it again. We can use our experiences, knowledge, lessons learned, business tools and wisdom to implement a successful change.

Example 2

Status quo language: This new change is going to require new and advanced skills, and it might drive me out of my job. I have seen things like this before and I'm worried I won't be able to keep up. I don't know why they keep doing this to us. I'm not going to be the first to comply. I'll sit back and act like I'm supportive, but in reality I'll be watching it all from my seat on the fence.

Willing and upskilling language: I know this won't be easy, but in the long run this new change will help us better serve our clients. Implementing this new process will help us eliminate inefficient ways of doing our jobs and help us build better systems.

This new Change will improve how we do our work. It will help us work smarter, not harder. This Change is not just our change. Most successful companies in our industry and beyond are faced with similar decisions. The question is, 'Do we "go and grow" or "stick with status quo?"' There are impacts for either choice. One choice leads to new opportunities, and the other may limit opportunities.

Example 3

Status quo language: This is probably a good time for me to take some time off. If I'm not here, they won't be able to ask me to jump in and help. I'm going to wait and see how this goes. Let's let others inside the organization figure it out first because it will probably fail anyway. Regardless, if this does go forward, it is going to be a nightmare learning this new system. It never works the way they say it will. Why can't we just leave things the way they are? Just when we learn a new system, it seems like they mess it up and try to implement something new. I fear what is coming next!

Willing and upskilling language: I volunteered to serve on the new project focus group today. I have some ideas that may be helpful, and I'm glad the organization has asked for our feedback. I was reading in our industry magazine that this new Big Change is one of many grand initiatives that will be impacting organizations in the near future. I'm going to take that free class on this new software so I can get a jump on this before the training. I have also been using the techniques taught at our recent training workshop and they are already saving me time. I know this Big Change is going to be a heavy lift for all of us during an already busy time, but I believe we will be a stronger organization as a result.

So, dear diary, that is what I will do. I am going to pay attention to the words and behaviors that are being spoken and demonstrated to take the temperature of our change-readiness culture.

Will our culture embrace and optimize this new change or are people locked up in the overwhelm and oppose stages of resistance with a focus on keeping status quo in place? I won't know unless I look and really listen. I have more work to do.

Solo and Accountability

Accountability breeds response-ability.

—Stephen Covey

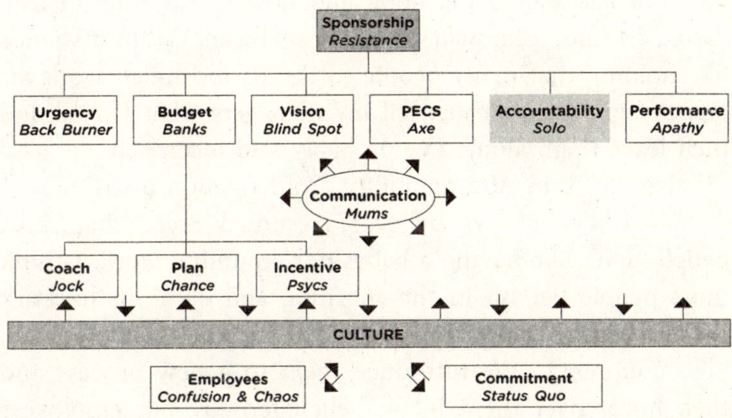

Day 20

Another meeting that occurred that week was between Accountability and Solo. The former lived near the park and was out for his morning walk before work when Solo caught up with him on the walking trail.

Solo said hello and Accountability politely responded. 'Mind if I walk with you?'

'Not at all,' replied Accountability.

They began to talk and soon the conversation turned to work. Accountability briefly recounted the death of Change and the introduction of Big Change.

'Wow, sounds like you've got a lot to do. How many people are in your department?' asked Solo.

'Oh, just me,' replied Accountability. 'I had two other people in my department, but I had to let them go.'

'How big is the management team?' enquired Solo.

'About forty managers and four hundred employees,' Accountability replied.

Solo had baited the hook and now it was time to fish. 'Look,' he said, 'I know it's none of my business, but it sounds like holding that many people to task is too much work for one person. I would just tell my managers what I need and then leave them alone. I've probably said too much.'

'No, no,' said Accountability. 'Your opinion interests me.'

'Well, I've always believed,' resumed Solo, 'that most people don't like having a babysitter around at work. I think most people get up in the morning and come in to work with the intent of doing a good job.' Accountability agreed. Solo continued, 'We introduce them to a new process and then hover over them like a helicopter. Are our employees not intelligent or competent? It's no wonder they are not more open to changes that come their way.' Solo could tell that Accountability was considering his words carefully. He went on, 'Take this Big Change for example. Why not just get him introduced and then let him do his thing instead of checking behind people everyday?'

'But that's exactly the issue that Agent had with me,' replied Accountability. 'He actually accused me of being a party to the homicide because of negligence.'

'He's pathetic,' said Solo. 'He failed at his job, so he just takes the shotgun approach and blames everyone. You had nothing to do with Change's death. You know your constituents, your managers and employees, and you were doing exactly what they needed for Change's initiatives.'

Accountability was a bit surprised at Solo's sudden sarcasm and his strong opinion. They walked for a while in silence. As they neared the end of the path, Solo said, 'You've got good managers. You said so yourself. Show them a little respect by not looking over their shoulders all the time.' As they parted ways, Solo smiled. He knew he was well on his way to doing his part for the Resistance Family.

Culture was not privy to the conversation between Solo and Accountability, but she sensed that when Accountability finally showed up for work that morning, something was amiss. She saw him miss several opportunities to get his team members 'back on track'. Reflecting on conversations with the now deceased Change, she recalled his passion for ensuring there was good Accountability. She wrote:

Dear Diary,

Change knew the value of Accountability. I remember him talking about the complexity of integrating Accountability with himself. He said that Accountability must be able to multi-task because there were so many levels where he was required.

First, he said Accountability must be present on a personal level. In other words, the employees must be motivated on an individual level to support the change. Also, there is a level of adaptability and reliability that must also be present for accountability to succeed at the employee level.

- **Motivation:** I believe that employees are more likely to be motivated to embrace change when they understand the big picture, have clarity about their specific roles, and can see the benefits of what the change will bring for them, their organization and the customer.

- **Adaptability:** To be adaptable is also important because Change will not be deterred. The speed of change is increasing rapidly, so it is important employees are competent in the present state and continuously build skills (with a forward-focused mindset) to be ready for the next future state. I believe Trainer is on top of this, but I will check.
- **Reliability:** Another critical component of our accountability success is reliability. Our organization's success during these ever-changing times depends on the employees to understand their roles, remain positive and adaptable, and complete objectives and tasks.

Making sure our managers are touching base with their teams in one-on-one meetings is very important. What questions do our employees have for their managers? Are we asking? What are their concerns and obstacles? I must make sure I get Incentive and Accountability together so we can do a better job here.

Next, Change had talked about the presence of Accountability on a department level, and then on a cross-functional level, and then an organizational level.

- **Communication:** For implementing change across the organization successfully, accountability must be seen, heard and felt in every part of the business. When messaging across the organization, utilizing key talking points and storytelling are excellent tools to help carry the desired messages forward. Stories of challenges, successes and triumphs can inspire and unite teams across the organization.

- **Collaboration:** Collaboration unites people and creates a spirit of we as compared to me. Collaboration within departments and even cross-functional teams builds relationships and camaraderie, and activates problem solving at a higher level. All of these benefits impact the role Accountability has on Change's success.

Sometimes Accountability gets a bad rap. What we are really trying to get to is for the employees to own the change and the new processes.

OWN
Contribution & Commitment Implementing the New Change Mastering New Processes ***Feels Confident & Optimistic!***

Urgency and Back Burner

A higher rate of urgency does not imply ever-present panic, anxiety, or fear. It means a state in which complacency is virtually absent.

—John Kotter

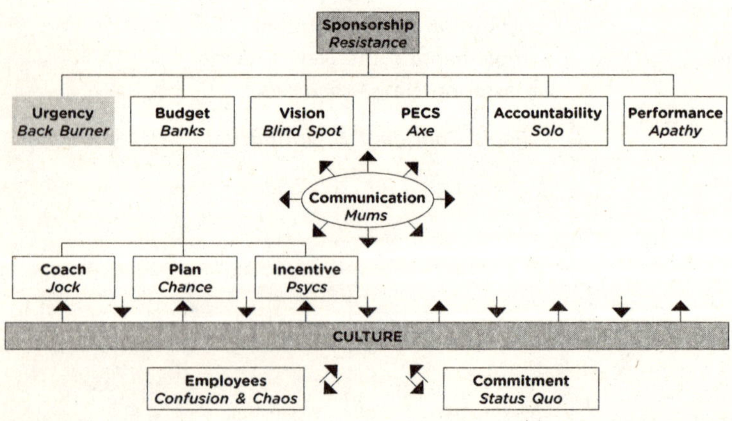

Day 21

Urgency and Back Burner had reservations for dinner at 7:00 p.m. Surprisingly, they both arrived on time. Urgency had made a renewed commitment to prioritizing his time since Change's death, and Back Burner did not want to blow his role in the killing of Big Change.

Unlike Vision who had to reach into her subconscious to recognize Blind Spot, Urgency was very familiar with Back Burner. He would not go as far as to call him a friend, but perhaps a casual acquaintance. They shook hands, went through the routine banalities of weather and sports, then ordered their dinner.

After the server had left, Urgency asked politely, 'So what's on your mind?' It was Back Burner that had invited Urgency to dinner.

Back Burner replied, 'I know this is none of my business and I probably shouldn't even know this but, you know, word gets around.' He had a worried look on his face as he continued, 'It's Big Change. I'm concerned there is not a sound business case for this Big Change and that he's coming too quickly given that another Change was just killed a few months ago. I read the Agent's report—matter of public record—you know. And I must say I do not agree with it, at least as it relates to you. I believe the business case you presented and the timetable you had to introduce and integrate Change was right on track. You had nothing to do with his death. If anything, he lasted longer than he probably would have because of you.'

Urgency was intrigued. He wasn't sure if it was because of Back Burner's seemingly intimate knowledge of his business or because Back Burner might be right and he had been too hard on himself about Change's death. 'So, what are you suggesting?' asked Urgency.

Back Burner was confident he had Urgency's full attention. 'Well, just this Big Change is huge compared to your recent Change. If your organization could not accept a smaller Change in the timing you orchestrated for him, and please allow me to reiterate I thought your timing was impeccable, how do you suppose they are going to accept Big Change so quickly? If I were you, I would pause… Well, I've said too much.'

Just then their dinner arrived. Back Burner began eating but Urgency did not even look at his meal. 'What would you do if you were me?' Urgency prodded.

'No, really. I've said too much,' replied Back Burner coyly. "You're the expert here.'

'Perhaps,' said Urgency, 'but I'd really like your thoughts on this.'

Back Burner put down his fork, wiped his mouth and leaned forward. He glanced to his left and right briefly to exaggerate an air of secrecy. 'We both know this Big Change is huge for the organization. We, I mean I, expect him to arrive at the front door of ACME organization in a limousine. When he gets out of the limousine, go out and meet him. Tell him the organization is not ready for him yet. Let him know someone will call him when the organization is ready. Now he may insist on coming in. His primary contact thus far has been Sponsorship, and he may not feel comfortable leaving without talking with him. If that happens, let him in but just walk him very slowly to the door. Don't let him come in too quickly.'

'So you know Sponsorship?' enquired Urgency.

'Sure. We play a round of golf now and again,' replied Back Burner. 'A good fellow and he usually doesn't talk about his work, but I think the last few months have been stressful for him. A round of golf loosens a fellow up and he spent nine holes telling me about Change and Big Change. But please don't let him know we've talked. Somehow I don't think he would appreciate people knowing he was discussing work matters outside the organization.'

Urgency nodded contemplatively. After a period of silence, Back Burner asked, 'How about some dessert?' Urgency had not touched his meal. 'No thanks,' he replied in a detached voice. 'I probably need to be going. Thanks for the advice.'

As he left the restaurant, he looked back at Back Burner who was with a waiter and apparently ordering dessert. He had been so confident about the Big Change but now after this conversation, well he had a lot of thinking to do.

Culture did not normally make a habit of exerting her influence outside the walls of ACME organization, but she had overheard the phone call in which Back Burner had invited Urgency to dinner, and she was intrigued. Sitting in a booth behind the other two, she had overheard the whole conversation. As Back Burner took his time over his dessert, she wrote:

Dear Diary,

This Resistance Family is cunning. They do not attack visibly but their approach is slow, subtle and cancerous. Urgency's main job here is to present the business case for Change. After Vision brought the opportunity to our attention, she worked closely with Urgency, who presented a compelling business case. It was compelling not only to the leadership of the organization but also to the line employees. The ability to accomplish this (I must give some credit also to Communication) is an art. Urgency was in rare form. He related this Big Change to the history of our organization. His message was evolutionary instead of revolutionary. He presented compelling data to support the Change, but he did it without the traditional power-point slides and excel spread sheet. He was masterful at telling stories about the organization and he weaved the data into the stories.

We cannot allow Urgency to backslide. If he begins presenting a case now of why Big Change should not come or not come now, the process will be sabotaged or at best he will be delayed and diluted. I will make an appointment with Urgency right away. I have faith that he will be resolute.

Another Change once told me that once you have made the decision to employ Change, be resolute in your decision but be flexible in how you implement him. Go to your employees and ask for their insights into the best ways to implement. He said, 'You don't want their buy-in, you want their involvement. The former focuses on whether you are going to employ Change. As the leadership team, this decision is yours. Involvement focuses on how you are going to employ him.'

Mums Silenced

The single biggest problem in communication is the illusion that it has taken place.

—George Bernard Shaw

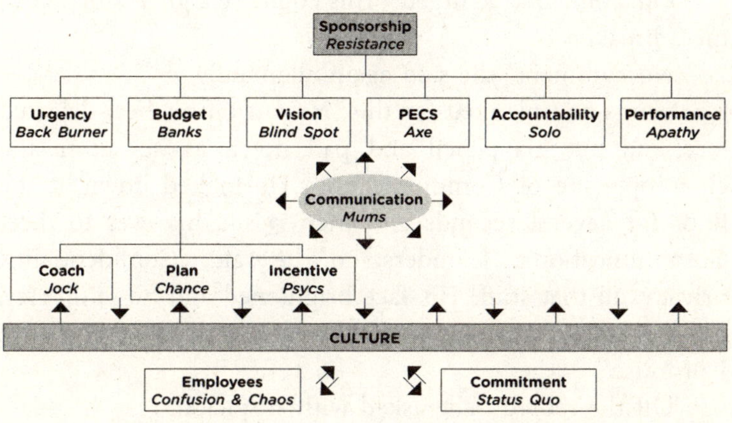

Day 22

Communication was in her office working, when she heard a knock on the door. 'Come in,' she said politely.

A very small man in a wrinkled, tan overcoat entered the room. He had a pencil and pad in his hand, and she estimated that he was in his mid- to late-twenties.

'Good morning,' he said cheerfully.

'Good morning,' she replied. 'How can I help you?'

Mums had practiced his introduction several times the night before. 'Name's Hadd, H-A-D-D. Ben Hadd. I'm a reporter for *The Daily News* and I wanted to see if I could interview you about Big Change.'

Surprised, Communication questioned, '*The Daily News* knows about Big Change?'

'Absolutely,' replied Mums. 'News is our business.'

She looked at him suspiciously for a few moments before saying, 'No comment.'

'Oh, come on,' he urged. 'This could be a great story. Give me a break.'

'No comment,' she said again adamantly.

Mums had planned for this. He put on his best-dejected face and put his pencil and pad down as he sat in the chair opposite of Communication. He looked down at the floor for several seconds and then raised his eyes to meet Communication's. 'I understand,' he said. 'Confidentiality, privacy, all that stuff.' His face brightened and he said, 'Hey, can I ask your advice on something? Purely off the record. I promise.'

'Off the record?' she asked with suspicion.

'Off the record,' he replied, picking up the pencil again and breaking it into two pieces. He interpreted Communication's brief smile as permission to proceed. 'This job is just temporary for me. What I really want to do someday is something like you do. I'm working on my master's degree in public relations, and we have an assignment I need help with. The professor has asked us to work with a local industry to write a communication plan. Now that the Big Change is coming soon, you must be in the middle of preparing a plan. I would be honored to learn from you. Of course, I'll remove all of the proprietary stuff, the name of the organization, etc. You can proof it before I turn it in.' Mums was pleased with his delivery. He had been humble and charming.

Communications said, 'Master's in PR, eh? A paper on a communication plan, hmmm. You must be in Professor Donovan's class?'

'That's right,' said Mums quickly. 'Good teacher. Drives you to do your best.'

Communication stood up. She was no longer smiling. 'Get out!' she exclaimed. 'I don't know who you think you are and what you're trying to do.' She pushed the intercom button and said, 'Get security in here now.' Looking back at Mums, she said, 'There is no Professor Donovan and…' Before she could finish, Mums had bolted.

Security got there quickly but there was no sign of the intruder. Mums had scurried up into another air duct. 'This is not good,' he thought. 'Resistance is not going to be happy.'

Culture was proud of Communication. She always knew that Communication had good intentions to support Change, but her health had prevented her from succeeding so many times. Culture wrote:

Dear Diary,

We must have healthy Communication with this Big Change, and I must admit that Communication's health seems to be improving every day. She is working harder than ever, and her listening skills have improved dramatically in the past few weeks. The other Change always said that the information associated with any Change had to be multi-directional, that it must be a dialogue, not a monologue.

Communication was out there every day. She was involved

in the announcement phase (worked closely with Plan on that) and did not disappear after this phase. I have seen her influence on posters, in the newsletters, at focus meetings, at departmental meetings, even in the suggestion box. The previous Change would be proud. I must encourage her to remain as vigilant during the implementation. She will need to work closely with Incentive, Performance Management, Accountability, Trainer, etc.

Commitment Questioned

Unless commitment is made, there are only promises and hopes...but no plans.

—Peter Drucker

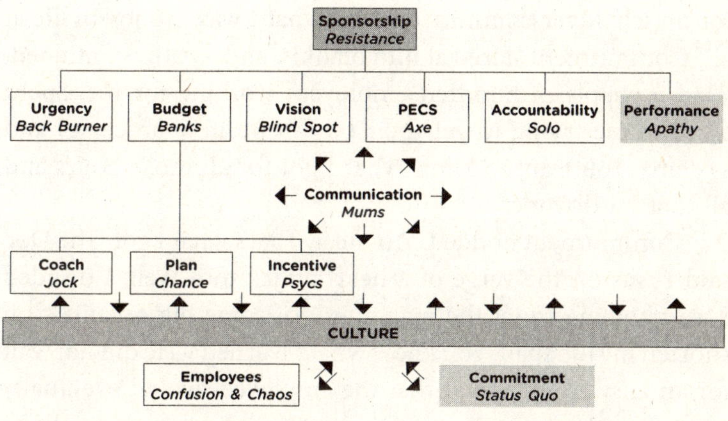

Day 23

During the last couple of weeks, Commitment had been working very hard. He had consistently put in 10–12-hour days. It was 8:00 p.m. at night and he was tired. He turned off the light in his office and made his daily walk to the bus stop. There was another man sitting on the bench. He looked shabby and dirty. Commitment concluded the man was probably homeless. He looked at his watch. The next bus was expected in about twenty minutes.

Their eyes met and Apathy moved down to the edge of the bench, patted it, and said, 'Have a seat. Take a load off.' Reluctantly, Commitment sat down.

'How's your day been?' asked Apathy.

'Fine. Long day but fine. And you?' Commitment said politely.

'Oh, just as happy as a hog in mud,' Apathy chuckled.

There was a period of uncomfortable silence. 'I used to be like you,' Apathy said knowingly. 'Worked all the time. No time for myself. Over-committed, that's what I was. No joy in life at all.' Commitment stared at him blankly, and Apathy continued, 'Had a couple of hundred employees working for me. Spent all my time trying to get their buy-in on new processes and systems. You want to know what I got for all those hours and all that hard work?'

Commitment nodded. 'An ulcer. That's what I got. The Doc said I was on the verge of a heart attack too. Well, I decided I wasn't going to let the machinery of some big organization shorten my life span. You know what I learned?' He did not wait for an answer. 'I learned that the employees would eventually commit without me nagging them. Might be sooner, might be later, but that was Urgency's problem, not mine.'

Again, there was an uncomfortable silence.

Apathy finally began again. 'Now don't think you are fooling me a bit. I saw the expression on your face. Seen it hundreds of times. I bet I can tell you what went through your mind. Homeless. Why doesn't he get a job? When was the last time he bathed? You're judging me on the outside, aren't you? You have no idea what I have on the inside. Well, let me tell you what's on the inside. Peace. Yes, I said peace.

Do you know what that is? When was the last time you felt peaceful? Do they pay you for all the extra hours you put in? Of course they don't, and if they did, you still can't buy peace. Why don't you stop spinning your wheels and enjoy life for a while? I bet you've got pretty good employees under you. Why not put a little faith in their abilities? Give them a little rope—a little breathing room. It would be good for you and them.'

Apathy got up as the bus approached. He turned to Commitment and said, 'If you died this week and one sentence could reflect your life on your tombstone, would it be "He was Committed"?' Commitment just sat on the bench staring blankly into the night as Apathy rode away on the bus.

Culture had been concerned about Commitment's long hours, and she was keeping close tabs on him. She knew that Apathy would make his move at some point, and she was strategically positioned behind the shrubbery next to the bench and heard everything. After Commitment boarded the next bus, she sat on the bench and wrote:

Dear Diary,

We do have faith in our employees. What does Apathy think he is suggesting? Integrating a new Change, especially a large one that crosses all areas of the organization, is hard work. I remember that simple model that I learned in college, and it seems appropriate to share with the leadership.

One night the professor communicated to us, 'If you want your employees committed to a change, you have to help your employees get it in their (he wrote on the board):

- Head,
- Heart,

- Hands, and then make a
- Habit out of it.'

He went on to explain it somewhat like this:

- **Head:** This represents logic. You have to help your employees make sense of the change. Answer their questions (what is it, why now, how will it affect me, and so on).
- **Heart:** This represents the emotional aspect. Employees have an emotional tie to routine. Help them understand that they are in a safe space with the change.
- **Hands:** This is the practical aspect to the change. You cannot make assumptions here. Help each employee understand his or her specific hands-on role in the change.
- **Habit**: You want the change to be sustainable. Stay close to the change. Measure progress and outcomes. Reinforce the processes and behaviors that contribute to the change success.

I will find a way to communicate this to leadership. We need Commitment more than ever.

Axe Cut Down

None of us is as smart as all of us.

—Ken Blanchard

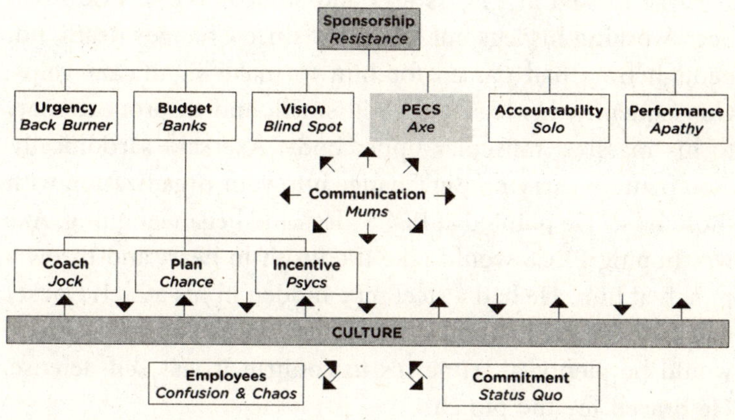

Day 24

PECS was in the gym doing leg curls when Axe came in. PECS finished his set and moved to the water fountain. When he turned after his drink, he almost ran directly into Axe.

'Oh, excuse me,' said PECS politely.

'No problem,' replied Axe. 'You were doing some pretty heavy-duty weights on those leg curls.'

Without any sign of embarrassment, PECS said, 'Yeah, thanks, I got a lot of work to do on my legs.'

'Is there a weight-lifting contest coming up that I don't know about,' asked Axe with fake surprise.

'No, no. It's for work.'

'Work?' questioned Axe.

PECS wiped his forehead with a towel and said, 'My main job at work is to carry Change out into the organization and we have Big Change coming in a few weeks. I'm just trying to get ready for him.'

Axe looked at PECS's legs and smiled. While PECS had been working his legs out feverishly since Change's death, not enough time had passed for him to make significant gains. Consequently, his legs were still small, and disproportionate to his massive, muscular upper body. Axe said sardonically, 'You plan on carrying Big Change into your organization with those legs?' He pointed at PECS's legs and began laughing. Axe was hoping PECS would take the insult to heart and throw a punch at him. He had a steel pipe hidden in his athletic jacket and had every intention of breaking PECS's kneecaps. There would be plenty of witnesses to confirm it was self-defense. He braced for the punch.

No punch came. To Axe's surprise, PECS began laughing with him and finally said, 'Pretty pitiful, aren't they? The good thing, though, is it's not just up to me to carry Big Change into the organization. I have a great team, a powerful guiding coalition, to help me. I used to think it was completely up to me. Now don't get me wrong. Ultimately, getting him out there is my responsibility, but I've recently learned it has to be a team approach.'

There were a few moments of silence and PECS said, 'Got to get back at it. Have a great workout.'

Axe was not looking forward to his next conversation with Resistance.

Dear Diary,

Axe and PECS could not see me from behind the one-way mirror in the gym. I am very proud of PECS. He represented us the way the team needs him to. In a big change, the leadership team needs to 'carry the change' out into the organization. That begins when we are unified as a leadership team. We have to be on the same page. One person does not make the change successful. The team's role includes:

- **Engaging the right people:** Leveraging employees' skill sets in the context of the change.
- **Making sure the goals are clear:** Without clear goals, we leave room for ambiguity and conflict. I am reminded of that saying that if you aim at nothing, you will hit it every time. We must know exactly what we are aiming at.
- **Ensuring there is a climate of trust throughout the organization:** I believe this is one of the most important things we can do. Cultures in other organizations tell me that this role defaults to the human resources department. This is short-sighted. We are only as good as our weakest link, so our communication and behaviors as leaders must be consistent with these types of changes.

Like PECS, we must exercise our 'change muscles' to get stronger every day!

A Chance Meeting

Failing to plan is planning to fail.

—Alan Lakein

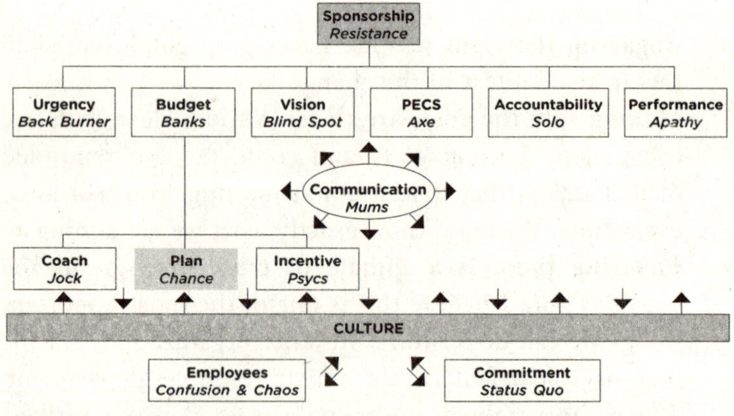

Day 25

By chance, he ran into Plan. Actually, that is to say it was a deliberate meeting orchestrated by Chance. He knew Plan was in his office preparing for Big Change. As he was about to knock on the door, it opened, and Infrastructure came out. She smiled as she passed him.

'Got a minute?' Chance asked tentatively.

'Sure,' replied Plan turning to the door. When he saw Chance, a puzzled look came over his face. He got up and met Chance at the door. Reaching his hand out to shake with Chance, he said, 'You know you look very familiar. Have we met?'

'I was about to say the same thing,' Chance said enthusiastically. 'Now let's see,' he said rubbing his chin and looking pensive. Finally he said, 'I've got it. The airport. That's where I see you a lot. At the airport.'

'That's it,' Plan exclaimed. 'The airport. So, are you a pilot?'

'No, no,' Chance replied with a deflated look. 'But I would like to be some day. I just love the feel of soaring above the clouds.'

'I know exactly what you mean,' Plan answered. 'There's nothing like it.'

'Hey,' Chance said as if suddenly struck by an idea, 'you wouldn't want to…no, it's too much to ask.'

Plan, who was always eager to talk with someone interested in flying, stated, 'Please, go on. Feel free to ask.'

'Well, I was just thinking,' Chance said conspiratorially, 'that if you had a little time, perhaps we could go up for a spin and you could teach me a few things. I mean, I know you're an expert.'

This was too much for Plan. He simply grabbed onto Chance and said, 'Let's do it!' He was so enthralled by the moment he never even questioned why Chance had come to see him in the first place.

Thirty minutes later, Infrastructure came back from lunch. She wondered what had happened to Plan. They were supposed to work together for the rest of the day.

Culture got a phone call from the lookout she had placed

at the airport. She knew the organization could not leave this Big Change to Chance. Plan would have to be brought back down to earth. She wrote:

Dear Diary,

We simply cannot allow our Plan to operate at thirty thousand feet on Big Change. He must be grounded. Our employees deserve to know what is expected of them and that requires tactical planning. That requires a roadmap, not a flight plan. We are good at developing our strategic plan for change. The leadership gets behind closed doors. We review our mission, vision and values. We complete our SWOT analysis and come up with our big plans for big change. Yes. That needs to be done. That is the job of leadership! But too often that is where leadership walks away.

We must get better at carrying Big Change out in the organization (note to PECS), but we must get more granular. These big plans need to be distilled down to the day-to-day process changes, a project plan that details the actions, the timing and the interdependencies. We do not need to tell our employees what to do. We need to engage them at this level. Certainly, we need to bring technical expertise to the table. That is a given. But front-line engagement, that is where we become successful. We cannot leave anything to Chance.

Culture called the airport. Their Plan would not be up in the air for long.

Jockeying for Position

In a world of constant change, the spoils go to the nimble and adaptable—those who can learn and unlearn with equal ease.

—Tom Flick

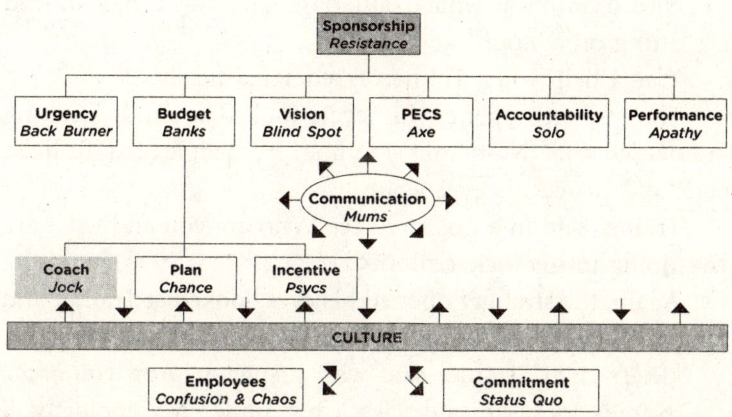

Day 26

Trainer (also known as Coach to everyone who knew him) was in the locker room getting out all the new equipment in preparation for the upcoming practice. He was in full uniform, had shaved, and as he passed a full-length mirror, he surmised that his diet was working. Trainer had taken Agent's words to heart. He had spoken with Sponsorship, and they were in alignment on what the players needed to do to build their skills. His job was to enable and encourage the employees, and he was taking his responsibility very seriously. Hearing a sound in the next room, he went to investigate.

When he entered the whirlpool room, he found a perfect stranger fully immersed in one of the whirlpools except for his arms, which outlined the top half of the rim of the steel whirlpool machine, and his head leaned back with eyes closed. Trainer supposed that was the source of the sound that had alerted him.

Next to him was what Trainer assumed was a glass of iced tea sitting on a stool.

'Can I help you?' Trainer asked sarcastically.

The stranger opened his eyes, looked around. Spotting Trainer, he said, 'No thanks. I'm fine.' He then leaned his head back and closed his eyes again.

Trainer said in a raised voice, 'Who are you and what are you doing in my locker room?'

Again, the stranger opened his eyes, looked at Trainer and said, 'Oh, I'm sorry. Please excuse me. You must be Trainer.'

'That's right,' Trainer said with suspicion. 'And you are?'

'Name's Jock,' he said with a big smile. 'My apologies. I didn't mean to invade your space. I didn't think anyone was here and I didn't think anyone would mind if I relaxed for a bit. Say,' he continued, 'why don't you join me. There's another unit over there and you look like you've been working too hard.'

'I haven't met you. Are you new here?' Trainer asked.

'Yeah. New. That's right,' Jock said deceptively. 'I have heard a lot of good things about you, Trainer.'

'Such as?'

'Well, they say you allow your players to do their own thing. That you recognize talent when you see it and that you go light on the training because you respect your players' talents and initiative.' Jock offered.

'Is that what they say?' Trainer asked.

'Sure. And I for one respect that philosophy. At this level of the game just let your stars shine, and others will follow the light. No need to overtrain, eh?'

Trainer said, 'And I suppose you are one of those stars?'

With a great grin, Jock replied, 'Used to be. You could say I've had a few good days.'

'And now?'

'And now I...' but Jock did not finish his sentence.

Trainer interjected with authority, 'And now you're a "has been" and a fake who has to prey on the weaknesses of others to get his jollies. You are nothing less than a self-perceived prima donna who wants to see others fail. I suppose you had enough core skills to excel in your—what did you call it—few good days, and you didn't think you needed to train. But guess what? You only shorted yourself by not reaching your full potential. That's not going to happen to my employees as long as I'm here.

'We take training and development seriously because we know growth is the lifeblood of our organization. We recognize that every role has a responsibility to contribute to their own growth, and this fuels our change success. We follow a simple model that has stood the test of time. It is called TRAIN.

'T is for *timely training*. Training must be offered before, during and after change implementation to provide the right information at the correct time. Sometimes organizations offer training months before a change arrives, and the new knowledge and skills are lost because it wasn't timely training. This takes us to our next important step.

'R is for *reinforce the learning.* Skills that are taught need to be put to use quickly. People learn when they can practice new ideas and receive direct feedback on their progress.

'A is for *accelerate and automate the pace of training/ education*. The more we can standardize our training processes, the better we build seamless processes for consistency across the organization.

'Jock, I can see that you are inching your way to the door. Hold on, I'm not finished. You need to hear about the secret sauce that is an important part of what we do. You see, it's not just about what we do, but how we go about doing it.

'I is for *innovating with joy.* Just like getting stronger in the gym, the same is true for learning new processes, new skills, and becoming a more competitive workforce. We celebrate these wins too and find the joy in learning together.

'N is for "*Be nimble!*" This is all about moving quickly and being able to adjust on the fly. This is why our sport teams continuously work on their agility drills. The same is true for the workplace. We need to welcome the mindset that change is ever-present, and we are ready to adjust where and when needed.

'So, Jock, we will always stay focused on development, coaching, learning and growth of our employees. We will never assume that we know all there is to know, and that we don't need to strive to get better. We all need to sharpen our skills wherever we are within the organization, and this is what makes our organization a winning place to work.'

With that Trainer looked at Jock, and for the first time,

Jock was actually speechless.

A few minutes later, Trainer eyed Jock scurrying from the locker room. 'Agent was right,' thought Trainer. He had advised Trainer to seek out his own personal trainer and that is exactly what he had done. His personal trainer had warned him not to be fooled by those who asserted that practice and training were not needed with Change. He looked at his watch and hurriedly headed to conduct the next practice session.

Dear Diary,

I am proud of Trainer in this encounter with Jock. Over the years I have learned many lessons (sometimes the hard way) about implementing Change, and a vital ingredient for successful implementation is led by my colleague Trainer. The important lesson I learned most recently is that Trainer may lead the charge, but training often involves everyone inside the organization. I believe for us to implement a successful change, there are responsibilities for leaders and responsibilities for employees that will help our efforts.

Responsibilities of leaders

- Leadership needs to be on board with training before, during and after implementation. This is another strategy like Communication where 'once and done' is not sufficient. As Trainer would say, 'Training needs to be Timely!' There are different training needs for employees and leaders during different phases of project implementation. For example:
  - **Before:** At the introduction of a new change, Sponsorship, Plan, Communication and Trainer must partner together to explain the purpose, the whys, the

expectations, the urgency, the desired outcomes, and the roles during change implementation.

- **During:** As the change begins to roll out, individuals will need training on new systems, processes, methods, communications, policies, etc. We must make sure that we allow for enough time to establish training in this important step.
- **After:** Once the new change has been fully tested and validated, bugs have been addressed, and old processes have been eliminated, it is time to create the reinforcement training for all new hires and existing employees who need training going forward. This must be continuously revised with updates, new process improvements and additional support systems.

- Trainer is a strategic partner in our implementation journey, and we will need a clear plan outlining the training steps above. I have noticed that in the past, when the reality of the day job becomes urgent, leadership has tried to shortcut the training process. This might include shortening the training significantly, excusing people from training, bypassing the training altogether for those who think they 'already know this information'. We will need leaders at all levels to walk the talk of value of training and recognize that this education we provide will aid in the adoption of the new change process. Leadership needs to participate in training alongside their employees. No one is exempt from sharpening and updating their skills. As an organization, it is imperative that everyone proactively works to improve their skills to stay current and relevant. It sends the wrong message when people are excused from training or skip it altogether.
- Leadership must recognize that there is a cost to training.

This includes the investment in educating internal champions/knowledge experts to teach peers and hiring external facilitators/subject matter experts. There is also the cost of people stepping away from their daily jobs to attend training programs—as well as the ramp-up time it takes to learn, practice and master these new skills.

- There is also a cost when organizations choose not to provide the necessary training required. This cost could be confusion, chaos, frustration and delay in implementation, a lack of buy-in, a failed initiative and turnover.
- When it comes to managing change, it is important that our leaders not only sharpen their technical skills, but also understand that there are many 'people skills' that are essential when leading during times of change. These important change-related skills include: helping employees' journey through the change process, calming the fears associated with the unknown, recognizing that the discomfort employees and leaders feel is temporary when learning new skills, and helping ensure that the Resistance Family does not set up camp in their department. Other essential communication skills needed by leaders are: listening skills, effective questioning skills, process improvement skills, change management and empathy skills.

Responsibilities of employees

- Do employees have responsibilities during change? I believe they do. This isn't something that is often discussed, but it should be. For this Big Change at ACME, it would be great if Trainer could help us educate our employees on the importance and value of how they can make a difference. Through our training programs, we could address questions, discuss the importance of mindset, reinforce the importance of continuous growth and development, and help them stay resilient as they learn and practice new techniques and implement new processes.

- I believe that an important part of ACME's culture has to do with the mindset each person holds, and how they feel about our organization. Certainly, I believe that the Sponsorship and our overall leadership team have great influence on the way people feel about the company, but employees still have choices to make about their own willingness to welcome the new change. Here are some questions employees may ask themselves during this training to provide insight and self-awareness.
    - Will I give this change my support? If I do give my support, how does 'support' show up in my behavior?
    - Will I be a positive vocal member, or more of a quiet fence sitter?
    - Will I volunteer to help and offer up my strengths, or will I let others do the volunteering?
    - When we are in the uncertain stage of new change, will I choose to be positive, or will I pick the more comfortable option of following the crowd of those around me? Did you know that it takes more energy to be positive versus negative? Positivity requires more intention and effort.
    - Will I be willing to speak up on behalf of the change when talking with co-workers? The role of the employee is very important, and through education and training, we can help employees realize how vital they are to the success of our organization.
    - Will I continuously improve my technical and communication skills and be ready for the next change

to come? Which skills will be the most important in the future and how do I strengthen those skills now?

As a summary, I want to reinforce the TRAIN model that will help us stay positive and be prepared and proactive in a changing environment.

T=Timely training. It is important that we pay attention to the different types of training needed when embarking on a change. The training that is needed at the beginning when we introduce a change is very specific to the audience: explaining what, why and how. Once we are midway through implementing the change, new training needs arise. Near the end of the implementation phase, it is time to ensure that refreshers, updates and onboarding training programs are created and ready to launch.

R=Reinforce the learning. To make sure that an initiative is successful, we need to have several offerings of communication and training. It is never enough to offer a training program one time and assume that the message has been received. For this reason, it will be important for us to provide many resources for our employees to learn, and to also measure results to confirm the transfer of learning. The many resources may consist of: messages from the CEO, town hall meetings and updates, virtual meetings, progress and status updates, question-and-answer sessions, experiential training, on-demand classes and support resources to reinforce the learning.

A=Accelerate the pace of training/education. People should not have to wait on the training. Automate development as much as possible and put training at employees' fingertips. In addition, it is important we teach our employees to adopt a 'process improvement mindset' across the organization.

If we are always making small improvements within the organization, this establishes an environment that welcomes change. These small but important efforts can be very helpful for minimizing the surprise and shock of a future Big Change. A great phrase for us to continuously ask is, 'What's new? What do I need to learn? What's next?'

I=Innovate with joy. Let's take the scary out of change and have some fun with it. Let's transform our culture into an environment of change agents. Let's find opportunities in our departments to make our daily jobs better. Even a small change can save us time, reduce steps, save us money which will allow us to better serve our clients. We must use technology to our advantage. We must remember to recognize those who are stepping up and thinking with an innovative mindset. Appreciation, recognition, feedback are all important factors that cannot be lost during the adoption of change.

N=Be nimble. Creating a nimble organization is continuous work. I have certainly learned this time and time again. Just when we think we have our Strategic Plan, or Training in alignment, the Vision defined, or our Culture humming like a well-oiled machine, something changes. But that's OK! Actually that's good. This means that we are on a quest to improve our performance, products, services, deliverables and organization at every turn. The days of coming into the office, doing the same job over and over, are over. We are flexible, nimble and resilient. Why? Because this is what it takes to thrive in today's marketplace.

And we are not going to let a one-time Jock with outdated thinking deter us from our mission to TRAIN and prepare our organization for change success.

Culture smiled as she wrote the last line to this entry.

The Family Plan

People don't resist change. They resist being changed!

—Peter Senge

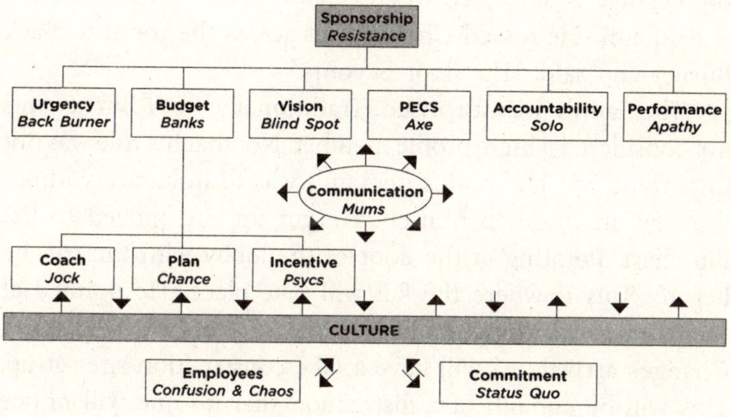

Day 28

The night before the leadership team would begin their two-day conference to finalize their action plan for the introduction and integration of Big Change, the Resistance Family gathered to review their own action plan. With the entire team there, except for Fear, Resistance called the meeting to order. 'With a few exceptions, I am very pleased with the work you've done over the past couple of weeks.' Mums and Axe did not make eye contact with anyone. The room fell silent when he said, 'I've met with Status Quo, and he has high expectations of us.' He moved to the flip chart and pointed at it with his bat. In it was a crude drawing of the front of a building. 'Plan A,' he said emphatically as he pointed at two large trees that flanked the lobby door.

PLAN A

'This is ACME organization. This is the front lobby where Big Change is supposed to enter two weeks from tomorrow at 8:00 a.m.' He tossed Chance's bat across the room to Back Burner and said, 'The floor is yours.'

The Family was surprised. Traditionally, Back Burner was not considered a high-profile member. Not that his role was not important, but his modus operandi was to influence without drawing attention to himself. He got up and moved to the flip chart. Pointing at the door of the lobby with the bat, he began, 'This is where the fall will take place.' He pointed at the two trees flanking the lobby door. 'On the morning of Big Change's arrival, we will have a fake construction site set up. This will be enough of a distraction that no one will notice the rope on the ground between the trees between the lobby doors. We will have a cable system set up and then Axe...' Axe stood up and flexed his arm muscles. 'Then Axe,' Back Burner continued, 'who will be hidden in these bushes will pull the rope, and this Big Change will trip and fall head-first into the lobby doors.'

Blind Spot asked without sarcasm, 'And we believe this trip and fall will injure this Big Change enough to keep him out?'

Back Burner looked at Resistance, who stood up and took the bat and the floor. He said, 'We do. We have calculated the size of this Big Change, the distance of the rope from the door, the hardness of the door. Oak, by the way. We believe Big Change will be knocked unconscious or perhaps even worse.'

The Family began nodding and murmuring their agreement and support of the plan.

'What we do know,' Resistance added, 'is that anything we can do to trip up a Big Change before he makes it in the door will either kill the change or render him virtually ineffective.'

The Family looked one to another. Some shook their heads. Others shrugged their shoulder. Blind Spot stood and began clapping, and one by one, the others joined in. Resistance held his hand out to recognize Back Burner who stood and gave a brief bow.

After the clapping died down, Resistance resumed, 'Plan B. While we have a high level of confidence that Big Change won't even make it through the front door, we think it only prudent to have a back-up plan. If he does make it in, we plan to use the C-15 poison.' He handed the bat to Blind Spot and sat down.

PLAN B

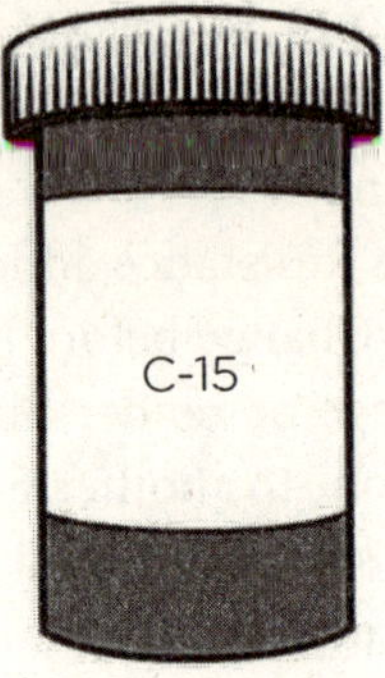

Blind Spot got up from his chair and began to walk slowly around the table. He looked more like a pirate than ever. He began to smile and a front gold tooth glittered even in the low light. 'That's right,' he said with a note of pride in his voice. 'C-15. It was good enough for other Changes, wasn't it?' As he slid his forefinger slowly across his throat as a gesture of death, the Family laughed together. 'It is a good poison but, obviously, we're going to need a much larger dose for Big Change, but I have to tell you, we have a very good start on that.'

Stopping behind Confusion and Chaos and tapping them alternately on the shoulders with the bat, Blind Spot continued, 'We've had a two-pronged approach. First, we take the heart out of Big Change through the employees and let me tell you that these two have already been very busy.'

Axe broke in, 'Wouldn't it be a better strategy to work on the leadership and management first?'

'Ah,' replied Blind Spot. 'A reasonable assumption, but look at it this way. The leadership and management might accept the Big Change but if the employees don't accept him, he's done for.

The fact that most leaders and managers do not consistently understand and practice this principle is a huge weakness of theirs.' Psychs winked at Blind Spot. 'Now remember,' he continued, 'I did say it was a two-pronged approach, and we have not been negligent in setting the stage for the leader's and manager's contribution to the C-15 poisoning. Let's debrief on the activity thus far.'

With a deliberate pause, Blind Spot stopped and took a long drink of water. Looking at Banks, he said, 'Banks, you did a beautiful job with Budget. I think she's ready to start writing checks left and right. And that "get out the Approved rubber stamp"...well, that was just brilliant!' Banks stood up, pulled out his wallet and started throwing dollar bills all over the table. The Family cheered.

Then Blind Spot eyed Chance, who had been periodically rolling his dice but had refrained from the usual emotional responses out of respect to the crew. 'Any chance we can keep Plan floating around in the clouds?' The crew roared. Chance rolled his dice, then said with menace, 'Snake eyes.'

Psychs interjected, 'And you Blind Spot, telling Vision she was mistaking her new sight for insight. Now that was just downright genius. You have dramatically shaken her confidence.' As the cheering resumed, Blind Spot smiled briefly, then held up a hand to stop the cheering.

'Reverse psychology.' Blind Spot said placing one hand on Solo's shoulder. 'Leading Accountability down the path to trusting his managers carte blanche when in fact his job is to ensure oversight of their work. I believe that deserves an honorary doctorate in psychology.' Blind Spot walked back to where he had been sitting and pulled out an official-looking paper from his notebook. Walking back toward Solo, he said in a deeper voice than usual, 'Because Solo has met all of the requirements of cunning head games and has demonstrated his ability to plant the seeds of doubt in a high-level management position, I hereby bestow upon him an honorary doctorate in psychology from the University of Resistance.' As Solo stood to receive his certificate, the Family began chanting 'Doctor, doctor, doctor!' Blind Spot tossed the bat to Psychs.

After the chanting had ceased and the room was relatively calm, Psychs said, 'And then there's Mums.' Mums resumed his previous pose of staring down. Just then Fear came through the door, took a seat, and offered a brief apology for being late. 'Now some might say that Mums has failed the Family. Was kicked right out of Communication's office.' Psychs allowed a period of silence and then resumed, 'But you know what I say? I say that if it weren't for Mums, we would not have learned about the Big Change until much later—perhaps too late. Mums, you've given us time to prepare adequately. Who of us has not failed in the past?' Mums's ears met with comments from the Family. 'Here, here', 'Absolutely', and '… second chances'. In a very serious tone, Psychs said to Mums, 'We still have two more weeks, and we need you.' Mums smiled and said, 'I won't let you down.'

Psychs turned to Axe and said, 'The same goes for you. You didn't take PECS down the first time, but you will have another chance. Understand?' Axe raised his eyes and began punching his left palm with his massive right fist. 'Got it!' he said. Turning to Jock, Psychs said, 'Do you still have your special bat?' Jock held it up. 'Good,' Psychs continued, 'you will have another opportunity to use it soon.' Jock smiled and began methodically slapping the barrel end of the bat into his palm.

'And last but certainly not least,' Psychs said, 'is our good friend Apathy.' He belched and the Family chuckled together. 'You did quite a number on Commitment.' Turning to Solo, Psychs said, 'Have you two been collaborating? Looks like we may have to get a certificate for Apathy too.' The Family broke into another round of clapping and Apathy waved a hand at them as if shooing a fly away.

As the clapping faded, Psychs returned to his chair and Resistance took the floor. 'Thank you for the hard work so far,' said Resistance. 'But we can't relax. Tomorrow's a big day. Get some rest.' As the Family began to rise from their chairs, Resistance turned to Fear, who came in late, and said, 'Do you mind staying for a few minutes?'

Dear Diary,

I know that as we get closer to the arrival of Big Change, the likelihood that Resistance will become more active will increase. We should monitor for the signs and symptoms:

- We will see increased criticizing and arguing.
- There will be questions about the validity of the change.
- We will hear that is too much of a departure from 'that's the way we do things here'.

We must keep our eyes out for:

- **Disengagement:** Our employees can be easily overwhelmed by the change. They can become unsure of their role and 'check out'.
- **Productivity:** Until the change has been fully adopted, productivity may slow down, causing the employees to lose faith in the change.

- **Avoidance:** Some employees may procrastinate or avoid the change-related processes and behaviors that are needed with the change.
- **Objections:** Some employees may voice objections or create barriers to the change.

If I look back at my diary over the years, I have likely written what I am about to write and I can state, with full confidence, I will likely write it again in the future. So, if you are reading this again, please do not mistake repetitiveness for forgetfulness. Instead, attribute importance to it. Here it is (perhaps again):

I believe that we jump too soon to label employees as resistors. I believe that many of these employees have questions and concerns that have not yet been answered or addressed. I believe they are better codified as anxious and reluctant. If we take the time and energy to try to answer their questions and address their concerns, we have the opportunity to convert what we have previously labeled as a 'resistor' into a champion for the change. So many times, these employees' questions and concerns stem from a legitimate need. These employees often understand the current state, what works now and what doesn't work. I must admit I have not always known this. As an evolving Culture, I have made my fair share of mistakes. Now, I will encourage my leadership to listen to these questions and concerns in the spirit of the greater good, the striving to attain a successful change and nevermore marginalize these important players in our change journey.

Fear: All or Nothing

You gain strength, courage, and confidence by every experience in which you really stop to look fear in the face.

—Eleanor Roosevelt

Day 29

After the Family had left and Resistance and Fear had freshened their coffees, they sat down across the table from one another. Resistance opened. 'Look,' he said. 'I'm going to be straight up with you. I can't afford for this hit to fail. There's a lot on the line.' He paused, sipped his coffee and then said, 'I met with Status Quo to get his advice.' Resistance expected some degree of surprise from Fear, but none came. Fear simply said, 'So what did he say?'

'He said that you have to be in this with us 100 per cent or you have to go.'

Again, Fear had no sign of concern or surprise in his voice as he replied, 'So, which one do you want?'

'I want you in 100 per cent.'

'Are you absolutely sure?' asked Fear.

Resistance looked stunned. 'Of course I'm sure. We've had this conversation, haven't we?'

'Yes, we have, but I'm not sure you know all of the ramifications,' said Fear.

'Ramifications?'

Fear looked thoughtful. He planned to weigh his words carefully. 'You will remember me saying that people need and use me in varying degrees. For instance, I know you've had some issues that I've missed some meetings.'

'And your showing up late,' Resistance interjected.

Fear smiled and patiently continued. 'I've been here as much as you have needed me until now. You need to know what you are asking me to do. Very few people can deal with 100 per cent of me. So far, you've only seen and used me in minor degrees, not more than 40 per cent of my capacity, and I think we can both agree that I have been effective. I must advise against your request, but I will not deny it if you insist.'

Resistance could not know that Fear had just met with Culture before the Family meeting. Culture had called for Fear. The call had not surprised Fear but what she said did. In her office, Culture poured a cup of coffee for Fear and herself, and both sat.

'Thanks for coming,' she had said.

'Not a problem,' he replied holding up his coffee cup. 'You call, I come. That's my job.'

There was a period of silence as they sipped their coffee, but it was not uncomfortable for either one. Finally, Culture said, 'Well, here's the thing. I've met with the team individually and collectively over the past couple of weeks. The bottom line is, "pause"...well...we don't think we need you anymore.' She had a look of anticipation on her face.

'You have a big change coming and you don't want me around at all?' questioned Fear. Culture carefully considered the way Fear asked this question. She recalled the first conversation she had with Fear. He had used two baseball batters as an analogy to describe how people use him for different reasons. He had said, 'One batter on deck. He only calls for enough of me to balance his confidence. He uses me as a guard against overzealousness.'

Interpreting her long silence, Fear concluded he was not wanted at all and began to rise from his chair.

'Wait.' Culture said emphatically. 'Wait. Let me state a request.' She felt confident she could speak for the ACME organization team. With a bit of a grin, she said, 'We probably need enough of you to keep us balanced. Perhaps you could hang around and if the pitcher is about to throw a "change-up", you could let us know.' She winked.

They both smiled widely now. Fear had got up and said, 'See you around.'

Meanwhile in this meeting, Resistance had been considering Fear's word carefully as well, while Fear was mentally recalling his recent meeting with Culture.

Finally, Resistance stood and said emphatically, 'All of you, 100 per cent, I insist.'

Dear Diary,

We must accept that some level of fear for employees is natural in an organizational change effort. The change could affect their livelihood, it could affect their position, their source of power, their relationships, and the list goes on. It is the fear of the unknown juxtaposed against the status quo even if the status quo isn't optimal.

What our employees need is psychological safety. They need to understand that there is a safe place for them with this change where mistakes are expected and allowed—without penalty. How can we do that?

- We can listen intently to concerns about the change.

- We can accept criticism in a spirit of hoping to improve the change outcome.
- We can focus on learning. We cannot always predict every obstacle or issue with a change. Every change has 'discovery learning'. We discover. We learn. But we do not penalize.
- We set up platforms for constructive feedback (public and private).
- We do not allow issues to fester. We address them promptly.
- We celebrate when we reach key milestones or even when we find a path around or through an obstacle.

With Big Change, we are asking some of our employees to significantly alter the ways they have been working, the work that has brought them success or, at least, stability in their lives. If we do not manage the emotions, the concerns and the questions about the change, we are inviting Fear into the organization. Also understand that even with the best mitigation strategies, Anxiety will be present. A little anxiety is manageable. But Fear…well, we all know what he is capable of.

Overcoming Resistance

There is nothing more permanent than change, and nothing that meets with more resistance.

—Unknown

Day 30

At 8:00 a.m. the next morning, there was a buzz in the break room where the meeting to finalize the plans for the introduction and integration of Big Change was planned. Culture took a mental role call of the participants. The leadership and management team were all there. She smiled counting off the additional frontline employees the team had invited. Having employees at these types of meetings was a new practice for the leaders and managers but they had unanimously agreed that it was the right thing to do. The Secretary had arranged for a large conference room with a conference-style table set-up and the other tables had been moved to the edge of the room. Culture recognized Fear although he was facing the other way. She came up behind him and said hello.

He turned and said, 'Good morning.' She took a step back. 'I'm sorry,' she said. 'I thought you were…' But the man interrupted, 'I know, I know, you thought I was Fear. Happens a lot.' He held out his hand. 'Name's Anxiety. Fear and I are first cousins. We look a bit alike, but we are distinctly different. He sent me to stand in for him.'

Culture shook his hand but still had a look of surprise on her face. With a wink at Culture, Anxiety said, 'Don't worry. I'm a big baseball fan, if you know what I mean.' Culture understood. She smiled and said, 'Glad to have you here. Make yourself at home.'

Sponsorship called the meeting to order, and everyone took their seats. He offered a special welcome to the eight employees. He acknowledged to them that having them here was a new practice, but they could expect it to be routine in the future. 'In these meetings,' he said, 'we have a no-penalty box rule. We want your honest input and feedback even if it's something you think we don't want to hear. Obviously, we endorse being respectful of people, but you can be confident that your input will be valued and there will be no negative consequences.' The leadership and management team nodded in agreement.

We believe this new Big Change that we have been discussing over the last several weeks makes a lot of sense and aligns well with our mission, vision and values. He nodded at Vision and Culture, both of who smiled. Culture spent a few minutes reviewing the organization's Values along with her epiphany on the need to bring them back into balance and relevancy. This was not news to the managers and leaders because Culture had shared the newfound perspective with each of them. The look on the faces of the employees, however, revealed pleasant surprise.

Sponsorship outlined a proposed agenda. With input from the team, it was modified slightly. Consensus was reached on the primary objective:

- To identify enablers and barriers to the integration of Big Change
- To create an action plan which:
    - optimizes the enablers
    - minimizes the barriers

The team decided to conduct a SWOT analysis, and the balance of the morning was spent discussing the strengths of the organization as it relates to Big Change. At noon, the team broke for lunch.

The meeting resumed at 1:00 p.m. Sponsorship kicked off the afternoon with, 'We've had some great discussions so far. I'm very pleased with the progress. We've fleshed out our strengths.' He pointed around the walls at flip-chart papers filled with the product of the morning's work. 'Now,' he continued, 'we need to be very honest about our organization's weaknesses in the context of Big Change.' Just then the break-room door swung open, and the Resistance Family filed in.

Both Resistance and Culture had been around for many years, so they recognized everyone in the room. Resistance Family and Culture's team did not have the same history and thus they were only able to see the person or persons whom they had previously met one-on-one. Anxiety began walking slowly around the table. Resistance did not recognize Anxiety although he knew he looked familiar. He was about to approach him and introduce himself, but Sponsorship continued.

'Urgency,' he said, 'would you mind sharing your thoughts on this?'

Urgency eyed Back Burner, who nodded approvingly as if to say, 'Now's the time. Let them know you're not ready.' Urgency stood and stated, 'There is a lot to be done, to be prepared for Big Change in two weeks' time. Multiple interfaces must be considered. I started thinking that maybe we should postpone Big Change.'

'That's right. That's right,' mouthed Back Burner.

Urgency continued, 'But I think we can do it. We can always find a reason to postpone a change, but I am confident we have enough momentum, resources and competencies to pull it off.' He looked defiantly at Back Burner who was open-mouthed and blushing.

Resistance glared at Back Burner, then regained his composure. He said to himself, 'It's ok. That's why we have Plan B.'

Budget offered, 'We need to list financial position as a weakness.' Banks, who was in a tuxedo, beamed. He was not positioned to see what was in the notebook that Budget surreptitiously opened and looked into for a moment. It was a photo of ROI. 'But not a weakness that we can't deal with. I've done some work and have determined that not only can we afford Big Change, we can't afford to *not* embrace him. But like Culture, I am resolved to a sense of balance in the matter. We must balance this change with our day-to-day operations.' Banks looked crestfallen.

Sponsorship turned to Plan and asked, 'Do you feel like we have given enough time in preparing for Big Change?' Chance had been rolling his dice around in his hand and now he began to move them more rapidly. 'Go ahead,' he thought, 'tell them you've not had enough time. Tell them that it's very complicated and there are so many details to take care of. Tell them,' he willed. Plan began, 'Well, this Big Change is quite complicated.'

'That's it. Go on,' urged Chance. He had taken Plan up in the clouds that one time and had assumed that that was all it took. Soon after the flight, however, Plan had recalled a previous conversation with Agent, who had used a flight analogy to convey that Plan had a primary responsibility in the trip, but he needed the whole team for a safe and successful trip. So, unbeknownst to Chance, Plan has sought input from Infrastructure, Prioritization, Accountability, Measurement and, last but certainly not least, some of the employees who would be directly affected by Big Change.

Plan continued, 'But we've done our homework.' Looking directly at his adversary, he smiled and said, 'We haven't left anything to Chance.' For the first time, Chance, open-mouthed, dropped his dice.

And so the pattern continued. An ACME leader or manager would convey a weakness related to Big Change and then would follow with a statement of belief that they could overcome the weakness, leverage a strength, find an accommodation, and so on. By now, Resistance's face had turned red, and he was sweating profusely. He was about to give the order to attack when one of the employees broke in. The employees had been sitting together, and Culture had noticed them whispering to one another as the leaders and managers had been talking. It was Barry who spoke for the group. 'Look,' he said, 'we've been talking, and I must tell you that we have had doubts about this Big Change.' Resistance took a deep breath. 'But the way all of you have approached this, the planning, asking for our opinions, the way you are relating to one another, the commitment to piloting, the communication platforms, well…' There was a long pause. 'Well, just know that we support Big Change.'

Just then the door opened suddenly, and a tall, dark, menacing figure entered. Culture surmised that the members of ACME organization could not see the man and they dismissed the open door down to a wind gust. The terror on the Family's face, however, told Culture that he was very much visible to them. Culture leaned over to Anxiety and whispered, 'Who is he?'

'That's Panic,' replied Anxiety. 'He's a first cousin of Fear but from the other side of the family, if you know what I mean.' Confusion and Chaos began running full speed, in opposite directions around the table. On the second circling they ran head long into one another. Panic was fully in the room now and the Family members with their eyes fixed on him, they all fled the room. Panic followed them.

Anxiety winked at Culture and whispered, 'Well I don't think you'll be needing me for a while,' and he left.

Dear Diary,

There are so many moving parts to change. Sometimes, it can literally seem like Confusion and Chaos have been untethered and are running around the room. That is, if we do not take the time to lead and manage the change. Perhaps the statistics have changed since I was in graduate school, but I remember that our professor reference several sources that reflected up to 70 per cent of organizational changes fail. I raised my hand and asked him to define 'fail'. Without hesitation, he spouted off:

- The organization did not reach the goals or outcomes it expected.
- The organization did not reach the goals or outcomes in the time frame it expected.
- The organization did not reach the goals or outcomes in the budget it had forecasted.
- The opportunity cost became too great to continue. That is, the cost in terms of resources—including

> losing personnel—was higher than the projected benefit.

It made me wonder. We have all of this information about leading and managing change and as time went by, I could not find evidence that the 70 per cent statistic had changed significantly. If we are going to move the needle on that statistic, we must have a better understanding of how to recognize and manage Resistance.

The Arrival of the Big Change

If everyone is moving forward together, then success takes care of itself.

—Henry Ford

Day 44

Two weeks later, Big Change arrived at ACME organization at 8:00 a.m. in a taxi. Urgency greeted him at the front door and ushered him in without hesitation. There was no fake construction site in front of the building. There was no hidden rope-and-cable system. There was no poison hidden in an alcove waiting to be surreptitiously slipped into his drink. Big Change was embraced by the leaders, managers and employees. That is not to say that the organization did not have more work to do. While most of the Resistance Family had fled the organization, Psychs and Axe, two of the most faithful of the Family, remained and surreptitiously created pockets of Resistance that the organization had to overcome. Over the next few months, Culture took the time to reflect on what she and her organization had learned about change. Instead of putting her thoughts in her diary, she decided that she needed to get the word out to other Cultures.

A Letter from Culture

Day 90

Dear Cultures,

I have been the Culture here at ACME Organization since day one. I am, in fact, a charter member. I am writing this letter in hopes that I may be able to help other Cultures out there. The perspective that I write from is one of humility, from one in which I have made plenty of mistakes and hopefully learned from a few of them. I did learn early in my evolution that the organization must adapt to continue to stay in business. Perhaps I could call that out as the first major lesson; that is, *the only thing that stays the same is everything changes.*

Change cannot be left to *chance*. It must be led and managed, not in a manipulative way but in a spirit of respect and understanding that we have a compact, an unspoken set of agreements with our employees. Big Change needs *sponsorship*. I don't mean a leader that shows up at the auditorium meeting to describe the change and then is not to be heard from again. It needs sponsorship that has the credibility and who continues to communicate the status of the change through its maturation. It needs sponsorship that can communicate the *urgency* for change. I don't mean urgency in the sense of 'it has to happen fast'. I mean urgency that reflects the business case for change. When I say business case,

I do not mean just the dollars and cents of the proposition. I include clear articulation of the rationale for change in the business case. The employees must understand the high cost of remaining with the *status quo* as well as the opportunities that will manifest with the change.

Big Change is an investment. We must make sure that we think through and plan for the costs. And not just money. We will be asking our employees to learn new concepts, migrate to new processes and adapt to new technologies. While that is happening, someone has to do their day jobs. Do not make the mistake of short-cutting training and education and do not overestimate the capabilities of your employees. We must all stretch some with a big change. But not too far. We must *budget* both our money and our human resources.

Find every platform to communicate the change. Employees will want to know:

- What is the change?
- Why are we changing?
- When will it happen?
- What is my role?
- What are the risks?
- How will I know I am succeeding?
- What are the benefits?
- What is the penalty/cost for not changing?

Be prepared to answer these questions and other concerns when they are asked. Be prepared to answer these questions and other concerns when they are *not* asked. What I mean by that is that some employees will have the personalities to ask these questions, but some will not. Just because the questions are not asked does not mean they don't share the concerns. Be sensitive to that. Understand your employees. Find platforms to communicate with all personalities without making them uncomfortable.

Keep the *communication* loop top of mind; that is, with every communication, there is a sender, a message, a receiver and a feedback loop. It took me too many years to give enough attention to the feedback loop. What I am really talking about here is listening. That is an important part of communication that cannot be minimized. As leaders and managers, we have likely spent more time in the initial preparation for the change, we have executed the planning process, and we are eager to obtain and track milestones and outcomes. But guess what? We must sensitize ourselves to understanding that others are hearing the change message for the first time. Listening takes time and true listening takes focus and energy. True listening is a gift that you can give to others. Not doing it is a primary mistake that I made for too long and I do not want you to make the same one. I read a book some time back called *What I Really Meant to Say! A to Z of Meaningful Conversations and Deeper Relations*. This book provided some very practical advice to me in my personal and work life. I encourage you to read the book, but I pass along a few of these 'A to Z's that I believe are pertinent to change:

- **Avoid assumptions:** We don't allow assumptions (unverified formation) to sway our communications.
- **Construct context:** We consistently provide the set of circumstances or facts that surround a particular situation and give meaning to it.
- **Express expectations:** We consistently set and communicate expectations of others so there is little doubt about what the goals are.
- **Frame feedback:** We consistently provide thoughtful, constructive feedback when required.

- **Jam judgment:** We consistently wait until we have all the information to form an opinion or response.
- **Listen loyally:** We consistently listen with a hunger and an intent to fully understand what the other party is communicating.
- **Query the quiet:** We have a consistent heightened awareness of periods of silence and consistently intuit its meaning when it occurs.
- **Risk recovery:** We have consistent awareness that we sometimes make mistakes and when we do, we offer a genuine apology.
- **Scrap scoring:** We consistently avoid keeping score in relationships and communications (one-upmanships).
- **Value the visual:** We consistently pay attention to our own body language and the body language of others and what that communicates.

I have also learned that we must have Accountability with Big Changes. I am not talking about accountability that brings about *fear* of some penalty or retribution. I am talking about the kind of *accountability* that informs the employees of what we need from them with the change. I am talking about the kind of accountability that supports performance standards that can be measured on a regular cadence. And when we fall short of those standards, we don't criticize, berate or punish. Instead, we encourage, analyze for root cause, then educate and train. And as our good friend and guru Ken Blanchard often says, 'The key to developing people is to catch them doing something right.' When we also give feedback for positive actions and behaviors, we develop trust with our employees and promote good performance. I feel compelled here to remind us all that this feedback should come from the right spirit. Otherwise, it will be perceived as fake and manipulative.

Search and find that thankful space in your heart and then catch someone doing something right.

I recently re-read my diary. If you were to read it, you would see an entry in my later years that references information from my college years that up to 70 per cent of large changes fail; that is, they fall short on meeting expected outcomes, time to complete or budget. I questioned that with all the knowledge and resources out there on leading and managing change. Why have we not moved the needle on creating successful change more often? The items that you have read in this letter speak to much of the opportunity.

The final item—consider it advice—that I will relate to you is not necessarily a new one, but I believe the terminology encapsulates the spirit of a major theme of successful Change. It affected me deeply after I received this anonymous poem from one of the employees here:

Our Work is Much the Same
Another announcement of pending change,
that's three, no four, this year,
and yet our work is much the same
somehow so hard to hear,
<u>their</u> words so empty and full of nothing
<u>they</u> don't even know my name.
But **we'll** dress it up and shine its shoes,
yet our work is much the same.

If <u>they</u> would ask, **we** would tell
to improve the bottom line.
But <u>they</u> only tell, so *we* don't ask
and pretend that things are fine.

We chuckle as our managers and execs
scurry from meeting to meeting,

then guest appear and demand respect
with <u>their</u> messages self-defeating.

You see, change **<u>succeeds</u>** on level ground
not on the mountain peak.
So why not join us way down here,
it's greener than you think.

We have thoughts, ideas, solutions.
We even have a name.
So, stand beside **us** and get to know **us**
if you want **our** work to change.

What I realized is that we took these change principles and liberally communicated them at the corporate level. Then, our leaders became knee-deep in the initiative. They spent an extraordinary amount of time deciding on the changes. Our managers were ankle-deep in. They were called away to meeting after meeting to discuss the change. But our employees? Our employees received the auditorium announcement where the leader stated: 'Here is where we **were** as an organization. Here is where we **are** today and here is **where we are going**—the Change.' Oh, and let me not forget that they received a little blurb in the newsletter on the change. Perhaps I have exaggerated a bit here. The point that I am trying to get across is that we did not historically do enough engagement with our front-line employees. You might as well post 'Our Work is Much the Same' on the walls of your organization.

This is what I have learned and here is the terminology that I referenced. **Sense of Agency.** We must do a better job of creating a sense of agency within our employees. The term is akin to stakeholder buy-in, but for me it goes much deeper. A sense of agency is a feeling that I am the one generating the action. How does that relate to Change, you may ask. We must engage our employees sooner and more broadly in the Big Changes. We must seek their expertise and their input. Sometimes, we must put our leadership or management ego aside and engage and encourage the ones that are closest to work, the ones who understand the current technology and processes, the ones who can ask the right questions and 'what if' scenarios, to become involved in the Change cycle early on. When we do that, we will benefit from their expertise, and they will likely develop a sense of agency that will hopefully be communicated to the other employees.

Epilogue

Day 120

It was not long after Big Change had successfully entered the organization that Culture found Resistance's flip chart. She studied the information and began to connect it to the graphs that she had embedded in her diary. As she connected the dots, she saw a pattern emerging that she felt was worth sharing with other Cultures.

Dear Cultures,

1. When Change is introduced, Resistance sends a shock throughout the organization. They structure their strategy and communication to try to **overwhelm** the employees so this change **feels like too much!**

OVERWHELM	OWN
Culture Shock Disbelief Denial 'Not Again!' ***Feels Like Too Much!*** ↓	**Contribution & Commitment** Implementing the New Change Mastering New Processes ***Feels Confident & Optimistic!*** ↑
Enter Resistance Family Fear Confusion Chaos Frustration Anger ***Feels Like Us Against Them!*** ⇄	**Willing & Upskilling** Learn New Skills Share Successes Lots of Communication Gaining Momentum ***Feels Possible!***
OPPOSE	OPTIMIZE

2. As Resistance gains momentum, their team leans into chaos, confusion and the perceived safety that comes with sticking with the status quo. As the organization attempts to move forward with the change, Resistance positions the employees to **oppose** this change, and that **feels like 'us against them'**.

OVERWHELM	OWN
Culture Shock Disbelief Denial 'Not Again!' ***Feels Like Too Much!***	**Contribution & Commitment** Implementing the New Change Mastering New Processes ***Feels Confident & Optimistic!***
Enter Resistance Family Fear Confusion Chaos Frustration Anger ***Feels Like Us Against Them!***	**Willing & Upskilling** Learn New Skills Share Successes Lots of Communication Gaining Momentum ***Feels Possible!***
OPPOSE	OPTIMIZE

3. Our Culture (me) and our leadership team recognize Resistance's strategy and work to help our employees understand the change, what their roles are, and provide the training and motivation for their success and our success. We work hard to help the employees to **optimize** their time and skills so this change **feels possible**.

OVERWHELM	OWN
Culture Shock Disbelief Denial 'Not Again!' ***Feels Like Too Much!*** ↓	**Contribution & Commitment** Implementing the New Change Mastering New Processes ***Feels Confident & Optimistic!***
Enter Resistance Family Fear Confusion Chaos Frustration Anger ***Feels Like Us Against Them!*** ⇄	↑ **Willing & Upskilling** Learn New Skills Share Successes Lots of Communication Gaining Momentum ***Feels Possible!***
OPPOSE	**OPTIMIZE**

4. In this Change journey, we are striving to help the employees master and **own** the new processes and roles, so they **feel confident and optimistic.**

OVERWHELM	OWN
Culture Shock Disbelief Denial 'Not Again!' ***Feels Like Too Much!*** ↓	**Contribution & Commitment** Implementing the New Change Mastering New Processes ***Feels Confident & Optimistic!***
Enter Resistance Family Fear Confusion Chaos Frustration Anger ***Feels Like Us Against Them!*** ⇄	↑ **Willing & Upskilling** Learn New Skills Share Successes Lots of Communication Gaining Momentum ***Feels Possible!***
OPPOSE	**OPTIMIZE**